T0156448

In Defence of the Letter Double-U

And Other Engaging Insights into the English Language

W . Whoolery White

IN DEFENCE OF THE LETTER DOUBLE-U
AND OTHER ENGAGING INSIGHTS INTO THE ENGLISH LANGUAGE

iUniverse books may be ordered through booksellers or by contacting:

iUniverse
1663 Liberty Drive
Bloomington, IN 47403
www.iuniverse.com
1-800-Authors (1-800-288-4677)

Because of the dynamic nature of the Internet, any web addresses or links contained in this book may have changed since publication and may no longer be valid. The views expressed in this work are solely those of the author and do not necessarily reflect the views of the publisher, and the publisher hereby disclaims any responsibility for them.

Any people depicted in stock imagery provided by Thinkstock are models, and such images are being used for illustrative purposes only. Certain stock imagery © Thinkstock.

ISBN: 978-1-4917-5490-0 (sc)
ISBN: 978-1-4917-5491-7 (e)

Library of Congress Control Number: 2014921881

Printed in the United States of America.

iUniverse rev. date: 12/15/2014

To
Willard the Wonder Weasel,
a cartoon character
who died aborning.

Contents

PREFACE

Enough is enough! For most of my adult life I have sat back and watched the most fascinating letter in the English alphabet misunderstood, maligned, and mispronounced. I have waited patiently for someone to come forward to defend the letter Double-U, someone with the empathy and passion to raise the clarion call, "Wake up all you English-speaking people! The Double-U is unique, vibrant and beautiful among all the other letters of the alphabet. And, you have relegated it to second-class status, in the alphabet's dust bin, in company with X, Y, and Z!"

Alas, no one has come to mount such a charge on behalf of our most complex, multifaceted, yet neglected letter. I have waited long enough for a "Champion of the Double-U" to press to the fore and lead the charge. The wait is now over.

I must now mount the charge myself. After many years of deliberation, I see that I am obligated to stand between my dear friend Double-U and those who pronounce it "dubya." I have no choice but to denounce all type fonts that represent my defenseless friend as Double V, rather than Double U. Though concerned that I might not be equal to this daunting task, I now assume the role of "Chief Advocate and Apologist for the Letter Double-U." Today I take my courageous and historic stand in the breech between "Dubya" and "Double-U." On this date, I raise a trumpet blast to call all English-speaking people to wake up to a new, fresh understanding of the majestic Double-U!

As you might surmise from my initials, I have a close, personal, life-long interest in the letter Double-U. I have had an almost daily relationship with a letter which has cast a long shadow across my years. That may sound a bit lonely and pathetic, yet hear me out. As a child entering elementary school as Wallace Whoolery White, I noticed many of my teachers quickly mentioned the unusual W.W.W. initials. That not only became for me a proud distinction, that set me apart from other kids with messy, less integrated initials, but gave me cover from having to constantly explain my embarrassing middle name. I was the only kid at Forest Lawn Elementary School in Marion, Ohio with the initials W.W.W.! Who knew but what I might be the only kid in the entire city!

For most of my school years I signed my name using the traditional cursive Double-V letter (*W*). Something apparently preordained occurred one day in high school. I saw a friend of mine write the letter Double-U in a sweeping, rounded-bottom, cursive more *UU* style! In an instant I was introduced to the full beauty of the letter which introduced all my names. I would never again return to using that misleading, deceptive Double-V letter in my signature. The cursive *UU*-style just felt right. At the time I didn't know why, but it somehow seemed more majestic and powerful.

In my innocence, I had no idea what all that meant. I had not yet discovered the ancient, worldwide, hidden conspiracy against my letter. I was on the way to seeing that the letter that was casting such a shadow across my life was, indeed, the shadow of a Double-U rather than a Double-V. That supernatural, cursive moment was the spark that would lead to the flame of revolution in the English alphabet that I launch in this book!

But, there was another catalyst for the brave step I am about to take. During the George W. Bush years, as governor of Texas and during his presidential administration, there was a malevolent reporter for the Fort Worth *Star-Telegram* who pushed me over the top. Molly Ivins, in her distain for Mr. Bush, launched not only an attack on the man but an assault on my now personal friend the Double-U. She christened him "Dubya." From that day forward that sacrilege would be on the lips of people across the English-speaking world, probably for all-time!

An added insult came during the transition from the Clinton to the Bush administration. News reports at the time claimed some outgoing administration staff members pried loose the Double-U keys from computer keyboards in the White House. The final irreverence! Not on President-Elect Bush, but on that gentle, unassuming letter that had served the Clinton White House staff so well over eight years. There was nothing left for me to do but to come to the defense of my friend, regardless of the likely social embarrassment or my possible shunning by friends and associates.

I ask all you readers to note this date on your calendar. This is the day when radio listeners will begin turning off their radio when they hear my dear letter defamed with, "You are listening to Dubya-P-T-Dubya, in dusty, downtown, Cretan, Wyoming." This is the beginning of the end of kindergarten kids concluding their recitation of the alphabet with "…S, T, U, V, Double-U, X, Y, Z." They will begin to gradually enlist in the rebellion by insisting it will be "…S, T, U, V, Double-V, X, Y, Z" until *every* English type font represents our favorite letter as a Double-U, rather than a Double-V.

You are now entering a process that will change forever your perspective and understanding of this precious, abused, near-forgotten letter. It will not be long before you will never again look at a Double-U in the same neglectful, thoughtless way!

Your challenge in this volume, then, will be to separate the wheat from the chaff, the clarity from the crap. I feel no burdensome responsibility to treat you, the reader, with any great love and respect. You have probably long been part of the problem. You are undoubtedly among those who have for decades carelessly degraded the exulted position the Double-U deserves. I assume you have meant it no harm. Most who are uninitiated in the wonders of the Double-U are simply unobservant. If you *have* actually held malice toward the Double-U, though, I would ask that you not continue reading my book. I will gladly refund the total cost of your purchase price. You may try to reach me at *slimchancecharlie@darkhole. com.* If your e-mail is somehow returned undeliverable, I would ask that you print it out, tear it up, and deposit it in the nearest vvastebasket, you Double-V lover!

Where my research actually does have some foundation, I have tried to be faithful in citing such in the "Notes" section at the end. For those of you whose DNA lacks a humor gene (and all of your family members know who you are, just ask them), I have provided the note "I.J.M.U.T.C." for you. This abbreviation is for "I Just Made Up This Crap." You chuckle-challenged readers may want to carefully read through the "Notes" section first, jotting down where the "I.J.M.U.T.C." bits will occur. You will then be equipped with a heads-up whenever query is about to turn to quandary for you.

From the outset I have found that the printing industry is hostile to the battle I have undertaken. You may already be tired of seeing me represent the letter *W* as "Double-U." I have no choice. My state-of-the-art word processing software has 122 font styles. There is not *one* that represents my favorite letter as a Double-U. All are double-V, even the script fonts. How am I to prosecute my case against the injustices perpetrated on my client without a single font which permits me to even *name* my client! Therefore, I am left with no choice but for a time to refer to our letter in question as "Double-U," lacking for a time a font with an accurate letter representation.

Bear patiently with me. The revolution we are undertaking may one day change the very nature of printing. If not that, at least it might make some publishers a bit nervous. But if not that, then at least it will call to task that one careless, walk-time radio announcer in Cretan, Wyoming. He'll never work in this industry again! Small victories. As General Harden Festoon, the War of the Revolution officer who defended Carbuncle Knob in the Battle of Tender Treats, once said, after seeing that several of the women tagging along behind his brigade were stumbling, falling and spilling the water jars, "I'll take small victories over one-legged camp followers any day!" (I.J.M.U.T.C.)

Let the revolution begin!

Chapter Won

Vowels, Double Vowels, and Semi-vowels

Have you ever had voice training? Or, have you ever listened carefully to the diction of a trained vocalist? Their vocal enunciation is basically a series of open vowel sounds, lightly interrupted by enough consonants to make the words intelligible. Why is that?

It is difficult to sustain a pleasing sound with your lips sealed together (as in the sound of an *m*), or your tongue cleaving to the roof of your mouth (as in the *t*-sound), or with a harsh gargle coming from deep within your throat (as with a q-sound). The sounds we create while lipping, tonguing, or gargling consonants are simply not very pleasant. Run through the consonant sounds aloud right now and listen carefully to the cacophony of abrupt, harsh, truncated noises which consonant sounds produce. If you are sitting alone in a restaurant right now, you may want to take this exercise outside. A sustained, full run of the eighteen consonant sounds will peg you as mentally challenged by all those at nearby tables. Merely making the *m*-sound a few times each day in polite company, though, will probably get you well into the first round of eligibility for Social Security disability.

But, wait! Go back through all the consonant sounds one more time and see if you discover two of them which do not require closing your lips, bearing your teeth, roof-cleaving your tongue, guttural gurgling, or hissing. I'll wait. Looks like the woman over at the salad bar is beginning to suspect you of a bit of mental retardation, so you may want to keep this exercise down a bit. Done? Did you notice that the Double-U and the *y* are open-throat consonants? Maybe they should be placed in a different category among the consonants? The sound of the *h* also comes close, but I've never been particularly fond of the letter *h*. It's just a bit too throaty for my taste. A kiss should never be accompanied by the sound of your partner getting ready to hack up a big one. If you want that kind of trauma represented in your list, then add the letter *h* to this special category of open-sounded consonants. But, fair warning, you *will* regret this decision later.

Consonants do have their function in verbal and written communication. They are simply much more pleasant on the page than they are to the ear.

Vowels, on the other hand, are the darlings of the ear. The open, sustainable sound of an *a, e, i, o,* or *u* make them the key to beautiful verbal communication. On the written page, vowels just lie there in their assigned positions, looking pretty, much like any other letter. But spoken, wow! They exude the beauty assigned them by God at creation. Vocalists have long known this truth and it is time we rank audience members catch on. Vowels produce those open-lip, open-throat sounds that make a language beautiful. You might say they are the French kiss sounds of English. It is nearly impossible to spit on someone while making any of the vowels sounds. You may want to try that futile exercise in the vicinity of the nosy woman at the salad bar. It should be equipped with a spit shield anyhow, so have at it.

Now, take a few minutes with each of the vowels, sounding aloud the various ways each can be pronounced. You will find that throughout this entire pleasant exercise, your lips will never meet. If they did, we may have discovered you have a serious speech impediment. You may want to have that checked out before you continue reading this book. Lips that touch during the sounding of a vowel will never touch mine.

Next, do the same exercise with the Double-U and the *y* sounds. How many different sounds do these two letters create, either at the beginning of a word or later in a word? You should have discovered the same phenomenon here. The lips do not meet in any of those sounds and the throat and mouth passages stay pretty much open. I'm convinced. Let's try to put these two letters in a different category a little later.

Did you mess around trying the letter h-sounds in this exercise? How did that work out? Got along pretty well until you came to the *ch* and the *ph* sounds, didn't you? Serves you right for doubting me. I'll be watching you during our later exercises.

Author's Note: *This book will require you to perform* <u>*many*</u> *spoken word exercises. The revolution I plan to wage on behalf of the Double-U cannot move ahead without your full, energetic cooperation. Battles are not one in the barracks. If these verbal exercises are too much for you, then you may have to leave the ranks of those of us who plan to move ahead at any cost. If you find you cannot pass muster as one of my readers, I'm sure your television set will be all too happy to welcome you back. But, after the revolution, when you are still mispronouncing and disrespecting the Double-U symbol emblazoned on the victory platform, don't come crying to*

> *me for reinstatement. You may not have even noticed the disrespect in the sentence above "Battles are not **one** in the barracks." If you didn't, yet still choose to move ahead with us, that will have to go into your permanent record as your first demerit. But, I'm glad you are still with us.*

So, what *is* a vowel anyhow? The English word comes from the fourteenth century Old French word *vouel*, which was derived from the Latin *vocalis* (*littera*), meaning "vocal (letter)," a letter representing uninterrupted voice or breath. Phonetically, a vowel is a speech sound characterized by voicing (the vibration of the larynx) and by absence of obstruction or audible friction in the vocal tract, allowing the breath free passage.[1]

A common dictionary definition is, "One of a class of speech sounds in the articulation of which the oral part of the breath channel is not blocked and is not constricted enough to cause audible friction; the one most prominent sound in a syllable; a letter or other symbol representing a vowel."[2]

In Modern English the generally recognized vowels are *a,e,i,o,u*. Just those privileged, select few. But, most of us were taught in the first grade that the vowels are, "*a,e,i,o,u* and sometimes *y*." English linguistic tradition has permitted us to include the letter *y*, on occasion, to stand with those proud five Letters-of-the-Open-Mouth. How generous of us to recognize that rare occasion when a letter other than those five serves the vowel function. But, wait, could there possibly be another one that deserves that distinction? Don't you remember a sixth possible vowel from your elementary years?

> ### *Are there any English words which contain all five of those vowels in order?*
>
> There are a few. *Abstemious,* an adjective meaning "marked by restraint;" *facetious,* meant to be humorous or funny; three rare botanical words, *acheilous, anemious,* and *caesious;* the rare zoological word *annelidous,* and the chemical term *arsenious.*[3]

The *y* clearly meets the definition of a vowel in many instances. In *you, yoke,* and *yonder,* the *y*-sound is "ee," the same sound of the vowel e in *even, equate,* and *ether.* In *my, try,* and *tyke,* the *y*-sound is "eye-ee." No blocking of the breath channel here. Both seem to meet the definition of a vowel. But wait. Do I hear a *double sound* for the *y* in those final three words? Would these words be pronounced the same if they were spelled *mie, trie,* and *tieke*?

The vast need in our language for vowel sounds to carry the meaning of the spoken word (and nearly all language is oral before it is ever written) requires not just single vowel sounds, but doubling up on vowels as well. Double vowel combinations in English are nearly limitless. For that matter tripling, quadrupling, and even quintupling of vowels became necessary as our language grew.

> ### *Is there an English word with five vowels in a row?*
>
> Yes, the British word for standing on line with others is *queueing,* pronounced "kee-you-ing."

5

Another term for these combination vowel sounds is *diphthong.* A diphthong is "a gliding monosyllabic speech sound that starts at or near the articulatory position for one vowel and moves to or toward the position of another." More simply, the pronouncing of two vowels together glides so smoothly together that it appears to be almost a single sound, as in *toy.*

Double vowel sounds and diphthongs have been part of spoken and written English since at least the time of our Old English language. English in those centuries was spoken with energetic inflections. This was due primarily to the distinct sounding out of both vowels in double vowel combinations. Each vowel in Old English words, such as *eart* (earth), *healfe* (half), *glaed* (glad), and *eornost* (earnest) would have been fully sounded. For example "glah-eed," for *glaed* (glad).

The letters *j*, *q*, *v*, and *z* did not occur in the Old English alphabet. Therefore other letters were used to record various spoken sounds. For example the *q* was represented by *cw*, as in *cwic* (quick) and *cwēn* (queen).[5] No, wait. The letter *u was* in the Old English alphabet. What is that letter Double-U doing in these words? It appears that it was serving as the first of a double vowel sound! ***Could it be that the Double-U has served a vowel function for many centuries?***

Wait while I alert linguists across the English-speaking world! While I'm gone, let's take a look at those terms "Old English" and "Middle English."

* * * * *

The Roots of Modern English

Just a brief look at how we got the language we speak and write today. Dating the various stages of development of Modern English is apparently difficult, because language historians can vary significantly in dates for the periods of our forbear languages. Margaret Bryant suggests the following timeline[6]:

> ➢ 3000-2000 B.C., Indo-European languages
> ➢ 2000 B.C. – 400 A.D., Germanic or Teutonic language
> ➢ 449 – 1100, Old English (spoken by various Anglo and Saxon groups)
> ➢ 1100-1500, Middle English
> ➢ 1500 – present, Modern English

* * * * *

…..I'm back. Over the centuries our spoken English has flattened and become rather bland, compared to Old English and Middle English. The lively sound of our language prior to the sixteenth or seventeenth century (especially in spoken Old English) has compacted, through our human tendency to make tasks easier. The sound of Modern English has become relatively dull and monotonous. It just became too much work to pronounce all the double/triple vowel sounds, if we could be understood by shortening the sounds.

Multiple vowel sounds in many Middle English words have been flattened to simple vowel sounds. Such M.E. words as *Heued* ("heh-oo-ed") has become *head* ("hed"), *tiraunt* ("tee-rah-oont") has become *tyrant* ("tie-runt"), and *earnynge* (ay-arn-ing) has become *earning* (er-ning).

The Great Vowel Shift
(or, Who Needs a Double Vowel in "Renaissance?)

Students of the history of our language identify a period of time during which there was a shift in the amount of effort given to pronouncing some double vowels. "Vowel shift" is a term in philology and phonetics for a process under which a set of vowels undergoes change. The term *Great Vowel Shift* is used for a number of long-term changes which affected the English vowel system during the 15th-17th centuries. Some long double vowel sounds were flattened and some close double-vowel sounds became diphthongs.[7] This shift occurred roughly around the time of Geoffrey Chaucer (1340-1400). Many Chaucer biographers, however, do mention that the noted Middle English author was not aware of The Great Vowel Shift going on around him because he was busy watching the workmen planting the roots of the Renaissance all around his modest London home. Determined to preserve the beauty of English, he demanded until his death that his name be pronounced "gee-off-fray-ee." He once dismissed a chambermaid for apparently calling him, "Geoff." She was later reinstated, however, when her persistence wore him down. She claimed she had not said, "Geoff," but had shouted, "get off!" [8]

There are endless theories of why such a lackadaisical treatment of spoken English would spread across an entire population. Was it laziness? Did too much mead thicken and slow the tongue? Were Shakespearean actors pressured into compressing their dialogue in order to get the audience on their way before the public houses closed? Each of those reasons might have contributed in their own small way to the Great Vowel Shift. I suggest that the strongest influence on the movement toward flattening of the double vowel sounds was the growth in opportunities for personal conversations as the Dark Ages ended and the Renaissance began. As Arden Lykens, the chief advocate of this theory, has written: "People had way too much personal time on their hands during the Dark Ages. With very little ambient light in their personal spaces (i.e. thatched-roofed hovels), they spent many hours talking only to themselves, sitting in the dusk and gloom."

One popular form of relief from the boredom was to sit in a circle and each family member would speak aloud in the dark as many vowel sound combinations as one could mouth, before the family cow mooed. If the speaker repeated a vowel combination, the other players could strike out across the darkness with oxen bladders filled with whey, (whose used-by date had expired) until the speaker was struck a sound blow. (Lykens suggests this might have been the earliest forerunner of *Scrabble*).

This family fun began to die out when fiefdom land developers struck out across Britannia heralding the advent of the *Renaissance* and demanding it be pronounced with a single vowel sound. By the time of chapter twelve in your high school English lit book, you will find that flattening all double vowel sounds had become *de rigueur* (pronounced "duh-riger") throughout the isles. [9]

The spoken English of Scotland retains some of the beautiful, multiple-vowel pronunciations of old. The rural Scottish dialects might be the closest we have today of hearing some of the pre-Modern English sounds. In America, the closest we can come are the Appalachian and some Southern dialects. The language in rural locations tends to change more slowly than in urban and metropolitan regions. The more isolated regions of the U.S. have kept alive many of the double/triple vowels sounds of pre-Modern English. Those Americans who speak a more "sophisticated" English often look down on our Eastern mountain cultures (of whom I am a descendent) and Southerners for their slow drawl. Just as those regions have kept alive the simple style of music from the British Isles, they have also protected and cherished some of the double/triple vowel sounds.

There was for several years a celebrity cook on one of the TV food channels who hailed from Eastern Georgia. She was one of the best exemplars of these retained pronunciations that I have experienced anywhere in the broadcast media. The quick notes I took from just a portion of one of her shows turned up these rich double-vowel intonations:

- "bray-yed" for *bread*. Both vowels were fully sounded.
- "fah-eve" for *five*. She finds two vowels where we have only one today. It sounds similar to the common Old English spelling of *feyffe*.
- "free-nd" for *friend*. Picks up both vowel sounds, while most today get just the one with "frend."
- "grah-heet" for *great*. Sounds both vowels, but backwards? This pronunciation is similar to the Old English spelling *græt*, which used the combined *a/e* vowel sound.
- "wah-ont" for *want*. Sounds almost like a double vowel, but is very near the sound of the Old English and Middle English spelling of *wonte*.

So, is there a point here? A couple. The sounds of English in prior ages were livelier and richer, due to the many double/triple vowel sounds. And, next time you are tempted to ridicule some of our Appalachian and Southern neighbors for their hayseed dialects, thank them instead for keeping some of that beautiful sound alive.

The Most Common Vowel Sound in Modern English?

So, may we now move on after this quick look at the range of vowel sounds and letter representations in English? Not quite. Bill Bryson in his book *The Mother Tongue: English and How It Got That Way*, asks, "What is the most common vowel sound in English? Would you say it is the *o* of *hot*, the *a* of *cat*, the *e* of *red*, the *i* of *in*, or the *u* of *up*? In fact, it is none of these. It isn't even a standard vowel sound. It is the colorless murmur of the *schwa*, represented by the pronunciation symbol [ə] and appearing as one or more of the vowel sounds in words without number. It is the sound of *i* in *animal*, of *e* in *enough*, of the middle *o* in *orthodox*, of the second, fourth, fifth, and sixth vowels in *inspirational*, and of at least one of the vowels in almost every multisyllabic work in the language. It is everywhere."[10]

The name *schwa* is derived from a Hebrew word meaning "nought." Rather fitting designation for the direction our lazy tongues have taken the sound of English, don't ya (*y+schawa*) think? When one listens to Asian languages, the lively, involved, inflective sounds we hear coming from the busy mouths of the Chinese, Japanese, or Korean, leave us tired and breathless. The flattening, nay the grunting, of many of our vowel sounds has left us with a spoken language that must be downright embarrassing to a self-respecting vowel letter. The proud *a* in the Italian name Amerigo (ah-mare-ee-go) Vespucci, the source of the name of our nation, must try to find a place to hide out at the annual Vowel Reunion. This after hearing us sing, *"Uh-mare-ick-uh, uh-mare-ick-uh, God shed his grace on thee...."* No vowel sound is free from the threat that we Americans (uh-mare-ick-uns) will flatten it at the first opportunity.

Though the most common vowel sound in English, the *schwa* has no representation among our list of vowel letters. To be fair, we might want to begin teaching our kindergarteners that the vowels are, "A,e,i,o,u, [ə] (pronounced "uh"), and sometimes y." If I were a vowel and had the chance, I might choose to masquerade as a consonant. Let someone try compressing me then! Well, wait. Maybe there is a letter that has actually pulled off that bit of camouflage?

Let's Review Those Vowels

So, we are pretty comfortable so far that *a*, *e*, *i*, *o*, and *u* are undisputedly the single vowels from which so much of the beauty of our language and our vocal music comes. We can also admit that there is need on many occasions to let the *y* jump in to enrich the vowel potentials of English. We can also see there is a nearly unbounded range of combinations of these five-and-a-half vowels needed to represent the limitless intonations of our spoken language. We can also now admit that our growing list of "acceptable" vowel letters doesn't even cover the most common vowel sound in Modern English: the ugly schwa sound. So, we can stop there?

No, there is something many linguists call the "*semi-vowel*." Could it possibly be there are letters which are normally considered a consonant, yet sometimes come close to serving as a vowel? Yes, apparently. The *Wikipedia* article about semi-vowels defines them: "Semivowels, also known as glides, especially in older literature, are non-syllabic vowels that form diphthongs with full syllabic vowels. That is, they are vowel-like sounds that do not form the nucleus of a syllable or mora; they are not the most prominent part of the syllable. They are normally written by adding the IPA non-syllabicity mark to a vowel letter, but often for simplicity the vowel letter alone is written."

Boy am I ever tempted to attach a I.J.M.U.T.C note to that definition! You see why you need me to help walk you through this gibberish? My research has convinced me that those who study our language in most depth are often the ones most unable to *speak* our language.

Semi-vowels are consonants which are sometimes used to represent a vowel sound. Why? Because the available vowels just do not seem to fit the need of the word as it appears in speech. The most common semi-vowels are *y* and Double-U. We have already seen the occasional appearance of the *y* in the vowels list, so we have already given it the potential of full vowel status in some cases. But now, we must deal for the first time with the Double-U as a potential vowel, either semi or whole. Let's move on to Chapter Tw and see if we can make some sense of where the Double-U fits in all of this classification scheme for consonants, vowels, double vowels, semi-vowels/glides, and diphthongs.

Before we do that, however, let's return to the heading for this chapter: "Chapter Won." It was important to get your attention from the very beginning as to the lack of appreciation we extend to Our Friend the Double-U. Not only do we misrepresent the

Double-U with a double-*v* in our printed alphabet, but we begin our numerals not recognizing the heavy load our friend carries here also. We begin pronouncing our numbers "won, tw, three….." But, we spell them *one, two, three….*." Shouldn't the first number be pronounced "own," based on its spelling? What gives?

A foundational understanding of English must be that spelling was rarely uniform throughout the history of our language until sometime in Modern English. Our agreed upon spelling for much of our written English today is the culmination of centuries of struggle by various spellings of a spoken word to become standard English. In times of few printed pages and broad illiteracy, various spellings were not much of a problem.

Variations in Middle English Spelling of Common Words

Here are some examples of spelling of common words (beginning with Double-U) by English-speaking people in the twelfth through the sixteenth century:

- *Watch* – wacce (most common), wecche, wach
- *Want* – want, wannt, wonte
- *Weather* – wedirs, vedirs, wedere
- *Way* - wey, wei, weg, weie, we
- *What* - whatt, whaut, hwat, hwet, huet, wat
- *Wild* - wild, wielde, wylde
- *Wood* – wode, wod, vod, wude
- *Wonder* - wonder, wounder, vounder, wondir, wunder
- *Worse* – wurse, wurs, werse, wers

You should notice the occurrences of the use of a *v* in place of a Double-U (as in *weather*), and the switching of positions in the Double-U/*h* combination to an *h*/Double-U (as in *what*). The long relationship of the Double-U and the *v* will be discussed in Chapter Sewen, and the flip-flop with the *h*, later in this chapter.

Let's take the spellings of our first numeral, for example. It has had dozens of spellings over the past seven or eight centuries. In Old English the number "1" was most often pronounced "ahn" or "own," represented by a variety of spellings. By the fifteenth century the pronunciation had become "o-oo-n" or "oon," again with various spellings, but the most common spelling being *oon*. Related forms were *oones* for *once*, and *oonli* for *only*. Included among those dozens of spellings were *won*, *wone*, *wan*, and *woon*. The curious outcome of these centuries of various spellings and pronunciations is that we have ended up with a spelling that seems to represent the most common direction in spellings (*one*) but have retained the less common pronunciation ("won"). Oones again the Double-U does the heavy lifting but gets none of the glory. Won't you join me in either beginning to pronounce this number as "own" or change the spelling to *won*? Where is your compassion? The Bible says, "A laborer is worthy of his hire." How long must the Double-U carry this word, without any recognition?

Don't get me started on *two*! In fact, I think I'll devote much of a chapter to that travesty. Please see "Chapter Five – To, Too, and Two." Will you help me in this mini-revolution: "Won, tw, three…?" It shouldn't take us more than a few hundred years to get all English-speaking persons on board.

Chapter Tw

Double-U: Consonant or Vowel?

I will grant you this. There are some among you who may recall from elementary school your first grade teacher adding the Double-U to the potential list of vowels in the English language. But, they probably did it with some fear and trepidation because they really didn't understand what they meant by that, and they probably couldn't come up with a quick example to prove their point. So, most of you have just moved along through life assuming that the Double-U is pretty much a consonant, and that's that. My response to your cavalier attitude regarding the function of my favorite letter is, how can you sleep at night!?

What is a consonant anyway? We have dug deeply into the role of vowels in written English. What about the role of the consonants, a group among which the Double-U has been confined?

By definition a consonant is: "One of a class of speech sounds characterized by constriction or closure at one or more points in the breath channel; usually used in English of any letter except *a,e,i,o,* or *u*."[11] But membership in the consonant class of sounds and letters is not limited to just the closed sound criterion. There is also a test based on position in a word. "Phonetically, the letters *w* (as in *win*) and *y* (as in *year*) are articulated similarly to vowels, but *positionally* (my italics) they function as consonants, initiating syllables and introducing vowels."[12]

So, we are to assume that a letter that "initiates a syllable and introduces vowels" is to be considered a consonant. Let's check that out with just a couple "legitimate" vowels. Under this definition, the following English words might qualify the *a* as a consonant: *aesthetic*, *airplane*, *aorta*, and *autumn*. And, these words might quality the *e* as a consonant: *earth*, *eight*, *eon*, and *euphoria*. Grab a dictionary and check out the other vowels and you will see the same predicament with this definition.

Why is it that none of these vowels qualifies as a consonant even though they meet the second part of the definition? It is undoubtedly because they all represent an open vowel sound at the beginning of the word, not the constricted sound of a consonant. Fair enough.

Did your brief trip through the vowel-spelled words turn up a real curiosity? Did you notice that in no English word is the letter *u* ever followed by another vowel? There might be some foreign-words-into-English exceptions, but words which begin *ua*, *ue*, *ui*, *uo*, or *uu* are essentially unpronounceable. Or better, there are no English sounds which require those written representations.

Let's now apply this definition to the Double-U. It is true that when used at the beginning of a word, the Double-U most often introduces a vowel. Scan your dictionary and you will see that in probably 90% of the Double-U words the second letter is a vowel. The only consonants which follow behind a Double-U are *h* and *r*, and very rarely, the *y*. While you have your dictionary open, browse a bit among the Double-U words, pronouncing the initial sound of the Double-U and the vowel. You will find that the Double-U sound followed by any of the trailing vowel sounds (including the rare instances of following *y*) is always a double vowel sound: the sound is never constricted or closed.

What does this mean? I means that the Double-U does not meet the two-part definition of a consonant. It never represents a closed consonant-like sound. And, it does not differ from the vowels in the manner in which it introduces other vowels sounds or initiates syllables.

This must mean that the Double-U has as much right to be considered a vowel as does a,e,i,o, or u. Wake up, English-speaking people everywhere, have we been misrepresenting the letter Double-U for generations, maybe even for centuries? Is the name we assigned this letter so many centuries ago a clue to the fact the Double-U is clearly a compound vowel, unique in its function among all letters of the English alphabet?

There are no Double-A, Double-E, Double-I, or Double-O letters in the English alphabet. Why? Probably because the doubling up of these letters with themselves or with other vowels pretty much catches all the sounds we have cared to make in spoken English. But what about the need for a Double-U letter? Probably because it is used to represent a distinctive sound for some people, maybe somewhere between the one represented by the doubling of the *o* (as in *pool*) and a single *u* sound as in *pull*. A sound that often comes at the beginning of a word and is not easily or faithfully represented by either the doubling of the *o* or by the single *u*. That particular sound will be the focus of the next chapter.

My tongue cannot make, nor my ear hear a distinction between the sound of the *oo* in *pool* and the Double-U sound in *water*. How about you?

Whatever that particular sound, in the early days of our language it seemed to be best represented by doubling up on the *u*. And, it was such a common sound in English that it must have been easier to just designate that sound with its own letter: the *W*. Not the *W* (double-v), but the *W* **(the Double-U)**.

(You will note that I have now found a worthy representation of the Double-U. This stylized version I'm inserting from outside my font selections captures the beauty and essence of my favorite letter. What's say I now use this exquisite, shapely rendering to designate what is so often shown as the deceitful W, the dread Double-V?)

Once this letter became part of the English alphabet, we had a unique, distinctive letter. One that always represented a particular sound, much like a consonant does. But one that always represented an open vowel sound, much like the other vowels. Our alphabet now had a letter that defied easy classification. A letter whose assigned name actually described its function. A letter that could introduce any other vowel, thus creating an instant triple-vowel sound.

The one limitation on this multi-functional letter was that it could not introduce its own forebear: the letter *u*! There may be only one word in Modern English, one that has long been part of the English language, one not borrowed from a foreign language, that follows the *W* with another *u*. What is that unusual word? Please go to Chapter Eight to find out.

Now, let's get to know the wonderful letter *W* a bit better and see if you have been pronouncing it correctly. See if we can't bring some new energy and life to the *W*ay you sound many of your *W*ords.

Chapter Three

Pronunciation of the *LU*

There certainly is a rather unlimited range of vowel pronunciations in English. Due to our infinite vowel sounds, we struggle to come up with vowel combinations to match those sounds. And, we forget from one word to the next what combination of vowels we used to represent a particular sound. Therefore we end up with a mishmash of spellings for word pronunciations. If there is one thing certain about English pronunciation it is that there is almost nothing certain about it. No other language in the world has more words spelled the same way and yet pronounced differently"[13] Consider the following vowel sound predicaments for those trying to learn our language:

- heard – beard
- road – broad
- five – give
- early – dearly
- beau – beauty
- steak – streak
- ache – mustache
- low – how

- doll – droll
- scour – four
- four – tour
- grieve – sieve
- paid – said
- break – speak

We challenge English-as-a-second-language students with a hodgepodge of similar spellings for very different spoken vowel sounds. The lively world of spoken English can challenge our ability to represent even our universe of flattened vowel sounds.

But, thank goodness for the stability we have achieved with our consonants. Or, maybe not. The constancy of English consonants may not be what we might habitually assume.

Our consonants which rarely vary in pronunciation (regardless of what letter follows them) are *b, d, f, h, j, l, m, n, q, r, v, x,* and *z* (I'll save the *w* for later in the chapter). An exception for *j* and *l* would be some words imported from other languages (such as *jai alai* and *llama*). Can you think of the one exception for *m*? It is when the letter is followed by *n*, making the *m* silent (as in *mnemonic*).

We have eight consonants that are less constant. They can be used to present more than one sound. Or in combination with another consonant, serve as a single sound. These are:

- *c*   Used to represent the *k* sound in *cake*; or the *s* sound in *city*; or the *ch* in *chin* (though curiously, this is actually a *t-sh* sound represented by the *ch*).

- *g*   Used to represent either the "guh" sound in *gate*, or the *j* sound in *germ*.

21

- *k* Is nearly always the sound in *kite*, though when followed by an *n*, the *k* is silent, as in *knit*.

- *p* Also mostly represents the sound in *post*, but when followed by *h*, is pronounced as *f*, as in *phone*. Do we really need the *ph* in English?

- *s* Most often just the common sound in *save*. But when it is followed by *h*, it has the single consonant sound of "shh," as in *sheep*.

- *t* Like the *p* and s, does most of its duty as the initial sound in *take*. But when coupled with a following *h*, it represents the single consonant sound in *the*.

- *y* We spent significant time in the last chapter examining the tasks we have assigned to this busy letter. As the first letter in a word, it usually serves as the *ee* sound, as in *young*. But masquerading as a vowel, it is equally comfortable covering the long *i* sound in *tyke*.

Why have I left the *w* out of this discussion of consonant pronunciations? Once again my favorite letter is unique among both the consonants and vowels. **The *w* always serves the same oral sound when used as a consonant, and always serves the same oral sound when used as a vowel.** No other letter in the English alphabet can make that claim!

How *is* the *w* pronounced in English, and how *should* it be pronounced? Bear with me here, and please let's watch over our shoulders for the Language Police, because they will not necessarily be comfortable with what we are discussing here. They have led a conspiracy against the long-oppressed *w* and we are about to spring her from their grasp. They will not be pleased. They may well drag us from our beds in the middle of the night and embarrass us in front of our neighbors, poking and prodding us until we shout, "Dubya! Dubya!" while holding our fingers in the sign of the Double-V.

Much of what we need to know in the proper pronunciation of this letter is found in its true, historic name, Double-U. A popular mantra of Zen Buddhism is, "You have heard the sound of two hands clapping. What is the sound of one hand clapping?" Seeing the several possibilities in pronouncing just one *u* might confound us into thinking that pronouncing a *double-u* could be almost as mystical as this mantra. Not so. The *w* is much more regular and easier to pronounce than its cousin, the single-*u*.

The single-*u* can represent a very broad range of sounds in English. Here are some of them. My pronunciation nomenclature here is from the old school. I've chosen not to use standard pronunciation symbols, just to rankle the snooty purists among us. If you wish to know the appropriate symbol for any of the designations I use in this book, simply consult the introduction section of a good dictionary.

First, the long-u sound of *rule*, *union* and *truth*. This same sound is sometimes also represented in English by *oo*, as in *tooth*, *booth*, and *loose*. Likewise, this same sound is at times denoted by *ou*, as in *youth*, *cougar*, and *wound*.

Try these other long-u sounds:

- bush
- cucumber (which includes a long-u and a *schwa* in the same word)
- futile
- humor

- pudding (though *puddle* has the *schwa* sound and *pull* has yet another sound.)

That different *u* sound is the short-u sound of *pull*, *wood*, and *book*. You may be one of those speakers who pronounces these two *u* sounds identically, such as *rule* and *pull* both rhyming with *pool*. If you do, please stop it! You are messing up my hypothesis here!

When the vowel *u* stands alone, or linked with an *o*, the range of sounds it/they can represent is rather astounding. Try this medley of *u* sounds:

- cup, cupola
- tub, tubal
- rum, ruminate
- lush, luxury (first u a *schwa*, second a long-*u*)

The range of sound combinations we can assign to the single *u* is *unlimited* (schwa), *huge* (long-*u*), even beyond *measure* (maybe a *schwa*, maybe a long-*u*, depending upon the energy you wish to expend in its pronunciation). But, is that also true when we double the *u*? Does the *w* just double the infinite span of possible pronunciations for this curious consonant/semi-vowel?

No, a thousand times no! When used as a consonant or a vowel, our pronunciation of the *w* remains consistent. Of course, *who* is to say when the usage of the letter is a consonant and when a vowel? Not me. **I believe it is quite easy to argue that the *w* is true to its name, and should generally be considered a vowel, and not a consonant**. But an apologist, an advocate is seldom objective. You will have to decide when the letter is used as a consonant and when a vowel. If you can divine a scheme that can be sold to the Lingua Dogmata, have at it. Try these words for example. First, is the *w* used as a consonant or a vowel? Second, what spoken sound does it represent?

- always
- twine
- work
- between
- wing
- where (spend some time with this one. How do *you* pronounce this *wh* sound?)
- owner
- show
- powder
- web
- whack
- wrangler (do you sound the *w* here, or is it silent for you?)
- wuthering
- bailiwick
- new (do you get a long- *e* sound here, or just the *w*?)
- newt (how about here?)
- swing
- away
- dwell
- ewe
- Gwen
- quick (no, wait, there is no *w* here! But it sure sowens like it.)

How did that work out? In how many of these words do you think the *w* is used as a consonant, and how many as a vowel? Beats me. How many variations in the pronunciation of the letter did you find? I only found tw possibilities. In *where* I find two possible pronunciations of the word, but the same *w* sound in both. With *wrangler*, I can't get a vowel sound, try as I might. It is silent. Bottom line, I get the same sound for the *w* in each word in the above list. What is that sound?

The sound the *w* represents is always an "ooo" sound, similar to the beginning sound in *ooze*, or *oodles*. *The Oxford Companion to the English Language* describes the sound as, "A voiced bilabial semi-vowel, produced by rounding and then opening the lips before a full vowel, whose value may be affected."[14] Try making that sound. Open the lips and say "ooo."

In his history of the English alphabet, David Sacks believes this sound, the sound of my favorite letter, may be among our easiest to make. "With no subtle tongue positioning, 'w' is one of the easier letter sounds for English speakers to say. Babies can say it ('wa-wa'), and many children and some adults may substitute it for the more complex 'r' sound, as in "Wudolph the wed-nosed weindeew."[15] He continues with his description of the sound we make for the *w*, "W symbolizes a sound that reaches back to the ancient Germanic roots of English. Technically, it is the voiced bilabial semivowel – one of two consonants (the other being Y) that sound through your open throat in much the same way as a vowel does. The term "voiced bilabial,"....just means that W uses your vocal cords and both lips."

The Semi-silent Semi-vowel?

That relationship of *w* and *r* is a fascinating one, at least for me. If you have read thus far into this book, you will probably find it fascinating, too. Could be that no one is actually reading this section of my book at this point, and I might just be talking to myself. In that case, I am here declaring my candidacy for the office of the President of the United States of America. I plan to run as "The Real W.W.W.," with my promise that every American home will have free *Y Fi*, if they will choose to consistently spell *Wi Fi* in this more economical way. Forget government waste of money! Just look at the careless, thoughtless waste of letters in our spelling. Please see chapter nine for more on this plank in my platform for President.

Anyhow, if you are still with me, we were talking about the curious relationship between *w* and *r*. There is a long-held concept among English speaking people that the *w* is silent in certain words. Here is a sample of those words:

--wrack
--wrap
--wreath
--wrench
--wrinkle
--write
--wrong
--wrought

This is curious. The initial letter *w* in a word is sounded before *every* vowel, before the letter *h* (more on that later), and before a *y* (as in *Wyandot*). In fact, there is only one other letter (other than vowels, *h*'s, and *y*'s) before which an initial *w* appears in the English language. That letter is *r*. What gives? And, it seems that the *w* is not even needed in these words, so why is it there?

It appears that it is because of what I just said above regarding the closeness in the sounds which these two letters represent. Look again at the list of *wr* words above. Practice making the "ooo" sound before beginning sounding the *r*. I'll wait. It is important that you do this exercise. When you are done, please put your head down on your desk, letting me know you are ready to move on.

Now, practice pronouncing those same words, sounding only an initial *r*, ignoring the *w*.

What we get in the two parts of this exercise is a very similar sound. In making the sound of the *w*, the lips never meet. It is a continuing, open, "ooo" sound. If we follow that sound with the *r* sound, the lips close just a bit, but also never meet. The sound simply moves from the middle of the mouth forward toward the lips. Practice that again with the list of words, noticing from whence the sound is produced in your mouth, and the position of your lips.

Why is this exercise important? Any suggestions? Have you been paying attention? This *will* be on your final. I suggest that the reason the *w* appears to be silent in these words is the result of our tendency to make pronunciations as easy as possible, resulting in simply cutting corners when we make certain sound combinations. The earlier examples we have had of this laziness in spoken language were the flattening of the double-vowel sounds to one vowel sound.

When we pronounce *wrack* properly, we can fairly easily sound the *w* then glide into the *r* sound. You probably found that to be true. But, we can save a bit of energy and breath by simply ignoring the *w* and going straight to the *r*. The end result is that both pronunciations sound pretty much the same. I suggest that in spoken English we have just chosen to save ourselves a small whiff of breath by ignoring the sound of the *w* and going straight to the *r*.

So, I raise the question, is the *w* silent? You see what I'm dealing with here! My favorite letter is out there busting its hump, across continent after continent of English-speaking people, and it gets no respect. All it asks is a wee bit of effort, a modicum of wind, to pronounce possibly the easiest sound in the English language. We place it before an *r* and what does it get? Bupkes! Join with me in proclaiming that the *w* is *never* silent, we are just too lazy to sound it when followed by an *r*!

Let's continue this discussion of the so-called silent *w* outside the box. Isn't it interesting that text appearing within a box, as above, is so much easier to read? You haven't notice that? Boundaries seem to make all things easier to live with (or within) and to digest. One of the problems with language is that the boundaries are so blurred.

Just as I so adroitly convinced you of the non-silent *w* as an initial letter before an *r*, my favorite letter begins popping up on the interior of words. And, the claim is once again made that the *w* is silent in these cases as well:

- answer
- sword
- toward
- two (*see Chapter Five for a discussion of tw*)

Take a moment and practice pronouncing the four words above. First, sound them as we pronounce them today. Then say the word, pronouncing the silent *w*. Not too hard to sound the *w* in these words, is it? Is it just the same old indolence that has led to the disappearance of that sound in words such as these? Let's see how those words appeared in Middle English, when most vowel sounds were still given their due.

Probably the most common spelling in Middle English for *answer* was *answere*. Other spellings were *ondswere*, *answare*, *onswere*, and *andsware*. Notice that the *w* appears somewhere in all of these spellings. It is reasonable to assume that the letter represented the pronounced vowel sound in each of these spellings. *Answere*, for example, probably embodied the word pronounced something like "ahn-soo-ware." A correct pronunciation of our modern spelling of the word would pay homage to a time when we did sound the *w*, making it "ann-soo-er."

There are so few audio recordings of spoken Middle English or for the transitional decades into Modern English, that it is difficult to tell what the word actually sounded like during those long periods of time. The one extant conical-shaped recording purporting to hold samples of spoken Middle English is owned by a cooper named Putter Lonigan, who lives on the Isle of Man in the Irish Sea. Though never examined by qualified linguists, Lonigan claims the recording contains readings by Chaucer of certain expurgated stories from his original *Canterbury Tales*....tales too ribald for his publisher at the time. In a story appearing in the April 12, 2004 Douglas *Dayntethis* (i.e. "dainties"), the weekly newspaper in the island's capital, Lonigan claims one of the tales on the recording is titled, "The Summoner Serves Notice on The Wife of Bath." The voice on the recording is significantly muffled, but it sounds curiously like Ronald Coleman reading from the *Kama Sutra*.[16]

Back to my point. The etymology of *sword* and *toward* turns up the same probable sounding of the *w* in the Middle English versions of these words. A common spelling of the former was *swerde*. Other spellings were *swerd*, *sweord*, and *suerd*. It is highly probable these spellings represented words which sounded the *w*. *Suerd* makes it quite likely, given the difficulty of even pronouncing that word without the *u*-sound.

Common Middle English for *toward* introduces us to a M.E. hyphenated word: *to-ward*. Other spellings were *touward* and *towart*. Again, these spellings seem to indicate an attempt to represent a spoken word which contains the "ooo" sound of either the single or double *u*.

Now, what were we talking about before we took this fascinating foray into the realm of the alleged silent *w*? Oh yes, the pronunciation of my beloved letter. I have argued brilliantly that the pronunciation of *w* is consistent and easy. That it is dependable and just a joy for your mouth. Just as I am ready to put this argument to bed, reality rears its ugly head and challenges my thesis. What about the pronunciation of the *wh* letter combination at the beginning of so many words in English?

This question is raised in Jeremy Marshall and Fred McDonald's fun volume *Questions of English*.[17] A reader asks, "I was taught always to pronounce the 'h' sound in words spelt with initial 'wh' such as 'where' and 'which,' and told that to drop it was uneducated. Is the widespread use of a plain 'w' sound a mark of poor education or just carelessness?" The editors' answer will lead us into one of the most interesting facets of spoken English.

"At the time of compilation of the original *Shorter Oxford* in the late '20s and early '30s, the editors considered that the / hw/ was used by a large portion, but not a majority, of educated speakers in England. *Everyman's English Pronouncing Dictionary* (1989 edition) notes that the /hw/ pronunciation 'must be regarded as increasingly rare.' However, this comment does not apply to Scottish or Irish accents, which are characterized among other features by the retention of /hw/.

Both the *New Shorter* and the current *Concise* are intended to reflect contemporary 'Received Pronunciation' (RP, in its standard form, not the 'marked' upper-class form), and they give /w/ rather than /hw/ pronunciations. The use of /hw/ in most of England is now distinctly formal and old-fashioned, and though it may be used in public speaking and singing, its ordinary use by a younger speaker of English might well appear affected or pretentious. It is certainly not a mark of education; more one of regional origin or social background."

The answer here reflects one of the true curiosities involving the *w*. Let's crawl back into the box and examine this fascinating social/linguistic phenomenon.

White or Hwite?

How do you pronounce my last name? Careful now. Pay close attention to the initial sounds you make when you pronounce *White*. You have pronounced it one of two ways. Those two ways are designed by one of two standard pronunciation symbols (take a look in the preface area of any good dictionary). The first is /hw/, a sound which is described in my dictionary as "/hw/ as in *whale* as pronounced by those who do not have the same pronunciation for both *whale* and *wail*. Some U.S. speakers distinguish these two words as \'hwāl\ and \'wāl\ respectively, though frequently in the U.S. and usually in southern England \'wāl\ is used for both."[18]

How about you. Do you pronounce *whale* and *wail* the same or differently? Try them a few more times and listen carefully to what you are sounding. Here's the really tricky part of these sounds. **If we pronounce *whale* or *white* by catching the *h* sound, we actually make the *h*** sound first, followed by the "ooo" of the *w*! Thus the pronunciation symbol \hw\. This sound begins back in the mouth with a bit of air, which we then blow out as we finish with the *w* sound. Something like "h-oo-ale" and "h-oo-ite."

"If we pronounce those two words by deliberately sounding the *w* first, we miss the *h* sound all together! Something like "oo-ale" (like *wail*) and "oo-ite (like *wite*)."

Catching both the *w* and *h* in these words requires a sound that is a bit tricky for us to make. In order to catch both of these sounds in sequence, the words would have to be pronounced something like "oo-hale" and "oo-hite." These pronunciations require considerable extra effort, which is not normally going to happen in regular vocalizing of such words. They require us to begin the sound at our lips, then thrust the sound back into our throat. That is a sound/breath direction that is rather abnormal in our language. I suspect that if I heard someone pronounce my name "oo-hite," I would do a double take. What I would hear most is the harder *h* sound. It sounds a bit like a stutter.

This *wh* sound can get mixed up with the "normal" *w* sound to the point of confusion for some learning our language. It can be a bit tricky for our children as well. I had a young friend who inserted the *wh* into the word *wind*. His pronunciation was always "h-oo-end," making it an onomatopoeia, the word pronounced imitates the sound the word represents.

Marshall and McDonald's answer to the question posed above suggests that how we pronounce the *wh* combination may indicate a social or educational class for us. I don't have a good enough ear for this sound to divide various speakers into such classes. I must confess, however, that time spent in this exercise myself has convinced me that I have pronounced my last name with the \hw\ sound, as "h-oo-ite." You don't understand how deeply guilty this makes me feel. Given my life-long romance with the *w*, it pains me to the core to realize that in pronouncing both my middle and last names, I have not given the letter its proper place of respect and honor in either. My first name is Wallace, however, so that proud and powerful *w* sound actually leads the way in my full moniker.

It is with some regret that I propose that we all return to spelling *all wh* words as *hw*. Sound aloud the following list of such spellings and see if you don't agree this change would facilitate our better understanding of the sound of these words. Such a change would also place the *w* clearly in the position of a vowel, not a consonant, thus adding to my claim that this letter should foundationally be considered a vowel:

-- hwat
-- hwen
-- hwich
-- hwo (a better spelling would be *hw*)
-- hwup (this is only one of two words in my dictionary which has a *wh* followed
     by a *u*.

> The other one is *whump*. This reinforces my point made
> earlier that a triple *u* sound in English is extremely rare.
> Doesn't this also argue in favor of considering the *w* as a
> vowel in nearly all instances?

Before we leave this topic of the *wh* combination, we must
address the messy business of the words *who* and *whose*. I would
rather not, but we must. It would appear at first glance that the
w in these two words is simply silent. The above discussion of
the *wh* combination does not seem to apply to these two words.
At first blush it would seem that these words represent a very
specific sound: "hoo" and "hoos." It does not seem possible to
get the *w* sound involved here in any way. But wait. Without
the *w*, wouldn't the first word have to represent the sound "hoe"
rather than "hoo," and the second word, the sound of "hose"
rather than "hoos?"

Maybe going back to the Middle English for these two
words could give us some insight. The most common spelling
in Middle English for the first word was probably *who*. But
interestingly, other spellings included *hwo* and *huo*, among
more than half a dozen other spellings. This would take us
back to the initial *h* sound followed by the sound of *w*. Try
pronouncing those two Middle English words. They both come
out a bit like the sound we make when we want the horse
to stop: "whoa." The modern word *whose* has a bit different
etymology. The most common Middle English spelling was
possibly *whos*. But, no spellings seemed to have represented the
\hw\ sound, as did a couple of the alternate spellings for *who*.
All the alternate spellings seemed to represent a silent *w* or,
possibly, an archaic sound that actually caught both the *w* and
h sounds, something like "oo-hoh." There's a sound you don't

often hear on the streets today! Your guess is as good as mine. I warned you in my *Preface* that my research for this book has been pretty slapdash. You want a project for after bowling or card club? See what you can find and let *me* know. You can't expect me to do all the work here! I've lived under the shadow of the name Wallace Whoolery for several decades. Have some mercy on me, will you!

While you're working on that, I plan to go ahead with some history of my lusciously curvaceous letter. How did the *w* come to find itself huddled among this cluster of more humble, less attractive letters we call an alphabet?

Chapter Fwr

History of the Letter Double-U

ɯ is a latecomer to the alphabet. It was descended from the Semitic (a subfamily of the Afro-Asiatic language family that includes Hebrew, Aramaic, Arabic, and Amharic) letter *vau*, also spelled *wau*. In addition, this Semitic letter was the origin of the letters *f, u, v,* and *y.* So the story of the *ɯ* is the story of these three other letters as well.

It all started with an Egyptian hieroglyph that depicted a creature the Egyptians called *Cerastes,* which resembled a giant snake or dragon. This mark represented a consonant sound roughly equivalent to our *f* and was also the forerunner of the Phoenician letter *waw.*[19] The *waw* looked somewhat like a cross between our letters *Y* (capital) and *t* (small). It ultimately gave birth to our *f, u, v, w,* and *y.*

The *ɯ* form did not appear at all before Roman times. Sometime between nine hundred and eight hundred B.C. the Greeks adopted the Phoenician *waw.* They used it as the basis for two letters in their alphabet: *upsilon* (*Y*), signifying the vowel *u,* and *digamma* for the *f* sound. The *digamma* did not make it into later Greek, but the letter looked like a backwards small English *f.*

Later, the Romans had no letter suitable for representing the /w/ sound. In fact, the sounds of *u*, *v*, and *w* were not systematically distinguished. Our letter *v* was used in Latin to represent the *w* sound. Context usually determined the correct pronunciation. As a result, the Roman capital *V* was pronounced both as a /w/ in words like *veni, vidi, vici*, ("way-nee, wee-dee, wee-cee") and as the vowel *u* in words like *IVLIVS* (pronounced "Julius.").[20]

So during ancient Roman times, *u* did the work of our *w*, serving to represent both the *u* and the *w* sounds. The Latin word *equus* (horse) demonstrates the *w* sound in its first *u* while the second *u* takes the familiar *u* sound.[21]

In the seventh century scribes wrote *uu* for /w/, but from the eighth century they commonly preferred the Anglo-Saxon runic alphabet symbol *wynn* (ƿ), also spelled *wyn* and *wen*. That alphabet became the common alphabet of Britain sometime in the early eighth century, after the completion of the Anglo-Saxon invasion of Britain. Meanwhile, *uu* was adopted for /w/ in continental Europe, and after the Norman Conquest in 1066 it was introduced to English as *uu* joined together as the one letter *w*.[22] The occupation by the invaders from Normandy impacted all society in England, including the language. The Norman double *u* was one small change.

Some of the cloistered Irish monks that copied Christian and other ancient texts tried to incorporate the Roman alphabet into the runic, resulting in the signs for *thorn* (Þ) and *wynn* (ƿ) in Old English. While the *thorn* became a *y*, the *wynn* was adapted by both the Celts and Normans as two *u*'s or two *v*'s together (*w* or *W*)[23]. By the fourteenth century the *w* had replaced *wynn*.

Outside of Latin and early medieval Romance languages, then, the sound *w* had thrived in the Germanic tongues of

Northern Europe. The Anglo-Saxons, who invaded England from Northern Germany (beginning in the late fifth century) often spoke this sound. Such common words as *wassail, weapon, witch, woods,* and *swine* arrived in our language during that period. Each clearly carrying the double-*u* sound.[24]

The *w* is the twenty-third letter of our alphabet but was the twenty-fourth to join our English alphabet, somewhat ahead of the final two, *j* and *v*. The Roman alphabet had only twenty-three letters, missing *w, j* and *v*. These final three came into general use during the Middle Ages or Renaissance. Their use and function were eventually spurred after the mid-fifteenth century by the printing press.[25]

Early printers sometimes used *VV* for lack of enough *w*s in their type. That may explain why my favorite letter is the widest of all our letters in standard typeface. It is more than just an *M* turned upside-down. The difference is that the *M* stands on two vertical legs, but the arms of the *W* in normal typeface angle outward, probably reflecting this early use of two *V*s by some typesetters.[26]

This adds just one more credential to the claim that my favorite letter is the most fascinating letter in our alphabet. It is large, majestic, dependable, and represents one of the easiest sounds English-speaking people can make. In the consideration of most, it can serve as a vowel or a consonant. And in order to fill all these functions, it requires the largest space of any letter on the page. See how embarrassed I would be if my name were Edward Earl Evans? Not much power and majesty there. One must be careful what triple-initial names we give our children, if we wish them to live a life of power and pride!

In summary, our modern *w* had its recognizable beginnings in the Semitic letter *vau* (or *wau*), which grew out of the sound earlier presented by the Egyptian hieroglyph *Cerastes*, then picked up in the Phoenician letter *waw*. The Greeks adopted that letter (which resembled our capital *Y*), adapting it for use in both their *Y* (upsilon) and *F* (digamma) sounds. The Roman (Latin) alphabet chose the *V* to represent our *w* sound. With the Anglo-Saxon letter *wynn* (ρ) we moved closer to our modern letter. But it was the arrival in Britain of the Normans from the continent that brought us the joining together of two *UU*s to represent the sound, which later became our single letter *w*. The letter probably has been in use generally in this form since about 1066 A.D.

Chapter Five

To, Too, and Two

One of my earliest memories of elementary school was my introduction to the rather confusing word trilogy of *to*, *too*, and *two*. We were taught that we should pronounce all three the same, and that we could ignore the *w* in *two*, because it was silent. Let's apply some of my apologetics so far to these first-grade instructions. How did we come to pronounce them all the same and is the *w* actually silent in the third word?

How did we come up with the "t-oo" pronunciation for *to*? Any fair musing on the word would tend to lead us to use a different pronunciation for *to* than we do for the other two words. We pronounce most English words ending with an *o* with a long-*o* sound. I can only think of one homonym for our pronunciation of *to*, and that is *do*. Can you think of others? I can't come up with any others. Call me if you think of some.

Nearly all English words ending in *o* require the long-*o*: *go*, *no*, *so*, *bio*, *condo*, *typo*, *radio*, etc. A final *e* is sometimes used to require the long-*o* sound (*toe*, *hoe*, *woe*, *aloe*, etc.), but that final *e* is probably not necessary for most of us to get the sound right. Why have we continued this peculiar pronunciation of *to*?

Beats me. I would like to think it was my first-grade teacher's fault, but she is no longer living to defend herself.

Hang on for a few minutes and I will do some research into this dilemma. While I'm away, check out the American "preferred" spelling of *judgment*, and the British spelling of *judgement*. My spellchecker just alerted me that I have misspelled this word. My word processing software will not rest until I go back and remove that first *e*. Not going to do it. If I've learned one thing in my many years, it is that if you open the door even a crack permitting your software to push you around, the "Check Engine" light in your car will begin demanding the same level of power over your life. Not going to let any of that stuff get started. (*Note to Editor: Please do not remove the first e in judgement above. I intended to feign ignorance there.*)

What happened to that middle *e* when the word got across the pond?! I have long been concerned, even agitated about this missing *e*. Shakespeare spelled it both ways in his plays. The British will use the *e*-less spelling on occasion. Yet, we Americans continue to insist on *judgment*. The rule some of us learned in elementary school was, "Use an *e* after *g* and *c*, when they are soft (e.g. *advancement, arrangement*), but omit it when they are hard (e.g. *segment, pigment*)." I have been unable to determine where that *e* went in Colonial America printing. Would you please check into that also while I am away. Let me know what you find. I'll judg the quality of your research when I return. (*Stage goes to black, insinuating the passage of time. Lights then come up slowly on a figure hunkered over a computer, sipping cold coffee from a chipped Toby mug.*)

I'm back from both the library and the Internet. I wish you could do some of this research on your own. My local public library only has the abridged *Oxford English Dictionary* and the print is so small I can barely read it, even with magnification. Fortunately the library at our local small university has the full set with readable text. Problem is I must hang around in the college library stacks to do my research. Have you wandered through college stacks recently? They are deserted! Nearly every student in the building is in the room housing the computer lab. (I had a young friend tell me recently that he had completed his bachelor's degree, never having borrowed a book from the university library. Just textbooks and Internet.) As a scruffy, suspicious-looking old guy, I'm sure I'm being targeted by the university library staff as a dirty old man, trying to look up the skirt of a young coed. I suspect that fear makes me look even more self-conscious and shifty!

When I was leaving the library just now, I just sidled up to the circulation desk attendant and said with some indignation, "You know, very few coeds actually wear skirts to the library these days!" The security guard that quickly appeared on the scene didn't have reason to lay his hands on me, so he didn't. But, he did follow me all the way out to my car.

So, I am forced to spend too much of my research time hunkered down in front of my computer, begging the Internet for information I would rather gather at the library, with real people around (regardless of what they are wearing). I am sure my wife thinks that all this time I am spending on the Internet must mean that I am a heavy user of cyber smut. I just can't seem to avoid being labeled a dirty-old-man. You have no idea what I have been going through just to scrounge up a bit of information for you. I just hope you appreciate it.

Anyhow, looks like our modern pronunciation of *to* is, as I suspected, a bit of an anomaly. It *is* one of the few words with a final *o* which we pronounce with an "oo" sound. Here's the story as I gather it.

According to the *OED*, in Old English the word *to* was pronounced with a long *o* sound, "like the *o* in *horn*." So, it was pronounced as "toe." But, the pronunciation of this vowel sound underwent a change during the Great Vowel Shift (fifteenth-seventeenth century). Remember that from Chapter Won? "Changes effected the sounds but not the spelling, resulting in the long *o* becoming the *u* sound, as in *moon*."[27] The question then becomes, why are *to* and *do* about the only English words with a final *o* that still carry that pronunciation today. We even correct the pronunciation for *do* when we double it to *dodo*. Incidentally, I didn't get any calls from any of you readers pointing up other final-*o* words that rhyme with our pronunciation of *to* and *do*.

There is one other etymology curiosity that I rather hate to bring up here. It just muddles our discussion about *to*. But, here it is. According to *OED*, one of the most common spellings during Gothic (or medieval) times for our word *to* was *du*, pronounced as it appears. So, during those centuries, one would hear either "toe" or "due" for our preposition *to*. That historic linking of the two words in question here is a bit ironic.

But, back to (or du) the general sound of the final *o* in Modern English. It would appear to me that it has undergone yet another vowel shift. We might agree to call this linguistic period "The Minor Vowel Shift Impacting the Final *O*," or *MVSIFO* for short. Notice if you pronounce this nonsense abbreviation ("miv-suh-foe") that the final *o* sound is inescapably the long *o*. Don't you think this rather proves my assertion that only our pronunciations of *to* and *do* have escape the phonetic ravages of *MVSIFO*?

So then, how shall we live? And, who is to blame for letting these two small words join our more modern pronunciations? First, I submit that we should all begin immediately the process of bringing *to* and *do* into the twenty-first century. I ask that you begin on this very day to pronounce them "toe" and "doe." It might seem a bit strange at first, but your family and friends will quickly recognize your wisdom and logic in sounding them in this way. If they don't, you may want to select other members for your family and a new group of friends. Incidentally, my moles in your region will be checking up on your pronunciations, and reporting back to me. We do know where you live. Please don't let future generations suffer the embarrassment you and I have endured pronouncing these two final *o*'s as either a *u* or a *w*. Centuries of wrong pronunciations can be corrected! Don't be a laggard. If we all work together, it will not take us too long toe doe this.

And whom do we have to blame for this linguistic failing? All of our first grade teachers! They were the ones who programmed us to believe that, "*To, too,* and *two* are pronounced the same, and the *w* is silent in *two*." Let's not let another generation have to labor under this archaic phonetic t*w*addle!

Other Words Which Begin with *TW*

But, before we go on, it's time for some more boxed text. Notice how your interest is heightened when we stick something in a box. Regardless of what the adventurous types say, most of us really do want to think *inside* the box.

There is a small group of words with an interesting sound. They are the ones which, unlike our spelling of *two*, begin with a legitimate *tw* sound. This is sort of the sound we make when we spit out a watermelon seed: "twa!" These are lively words for both the lips and tongue. They combine the tongue exploding behind the teeth with the following soothing, quieting sound of the *w*. This list includes only about two or three dozen such words, but they are among the most fun English words to pronounce. Words like: *twain, twang, tweet, tweezers, twine, twixt,* and *twit*. Go ahead.

Say these words aloud, with energy, and see if they are not an effervescent refreshment for your mouth.

None of these words would work with such gusto with another sound than the *w*. *Tuain, tooang, toueet, tooit*? Nope, just doesn't do it. When you want the very best in mouth refreshing sounds, reach for a *w*.

Now, let's move on to the second word in this elementary school chestnut. It gets easier now, since the remainder of these pronunciations are correct. *Too* is pretty simple. No problem in sounding this word, nor in understanding the sound it is written to represent. In Old English, however, this word was also spelled *to*. When used as a preposition, that word was pronounced "toe." When used as an adverb to mean, "to an excessive degree," it was pronounced as the stressed form of *to* ("toe") and sounded as "too." Sometime in the sixteenth century people began spelling it *too*, toe more clearly represent the sound they were making.

How about *two*? What's the story with the word for our second numeral? In Old English the feminine form of the word was *twa* (pronounced as it looks), and the neuter form was *tu*, which used our Modern English pronunciation for the word. The most common Middle English spelling was *tuo*, with other spellings of *twa*, *tua*, *tu*, *towe*, and *two*. The pronunciation of those words, in order, would have been something like "too-oh," "t-oo-ah," "too," "toe-oo-ee," and "t-woo." Obviously the spelling which won out over time was *two*. But, how about the pronunciation? Is it the same as the sound of *too*? If *twa* is pronounced "t-oo-ah," why is *two* not pronounced "t-woo," as in the famous line from the cult film *Blazing Saddles*, "It's twoo, it's twoo!" ("It's true, it's true!")?

The pronunciation guide in nearly all dictionaries has the word pronounced "tu" as if it were spelled either *too* or *tu*. The accepted pronunciation of *two* does catch the sound of the *w*, or at least, a single *u*. Curious thing, though, only one of the above Middle English words or pronunciations for the second numeral includes an *o* sound, and that is *towe*, a now archaic spelling and sound. So what does that mean? It means that the *w* in *two* is not the silent letter, the *o* is! We could spell the word *tw* and elicit the same pronunciation we use for *two*. Ipso facto, given what we have learned about these three words, we must revisit and revise our first grade dictum.

We must ask our early elementary teachers to begin using the following for these three so-called homonyms: "*To* (pronounced "toe") does not sound like *too* or *two*, and the *o* in *two* is silent." This minor adjustment in our early reader's understanding of the role and sound of the *w* will contribute greatly to his future mental health and well-being. Who knows how bright and articulate President Dubya might have been had he had the benefit of this early insight into his beloved middle initial?

Chapter Six

You, Yew, and Ewe

The Ames Brothers recorded a popular romantic ditty in the '50s titled *You, You, You.* When they sang that song, we knew which of the three homonyms were being used in their lyrics. There was no confusion that they might have been singing, "You, ewe, yew, I'm in love with you, ewe, yew." How could we be so certain? The sounds of the three words are essentially identical.

Human language, of course, is foundationally oral and secondarily written. The sounds humans make to communicate and identify objects and concepts happen before we take time to try to figure out how to recreate that sound on paper in the form of pictures or letters. Some languages in fact never get to the stage of creating a written form of the spoken terms. One such example was the now extinct language know as Dunquat, a spoken dialect of a small tribe in the Amazon coastal region of Brazil.[28]

The little known and seldom researched tongue (of which only I have knowledge) was a dialect of the ancient Tupi language, from which also grew Reengage, the predominate language of the region today. It appears that spoken Dunquat consisted of among the fewest sounds ever known in human language. My research has shown that the small, remote tribe who created this dialect was habitual users of a local psychedelic plant, known in Dunquat as *"whoa"!* (as close as I can come to a phonetic spelling of their spoken sound). The daily use of this narcotic plant by all members of the tribe led to both unabated inbreeding within the small clan and a tendency toward frenzied outbursts of ecstatic shouting and crying aloud. Brazilian dialect specialist Espirito Labato, after decades of research among descendents of this tribe, could identify only four spoken sounds among the people group. These four oral clamorings had to serve the entire range of their verbal communication. Two of those four "words" and just a few of their apparent various meanings were:

- *Zounds* – "We can't be out, I cut some yesterday;" "Is that your hand in mouth or did I just eat another monkey?;" "Your dugout canoe is crawling back down to the river again;" and "My smallest child could whip your old lady!"
- *Payeeote*- "While you're up, will you bring me a branch?;" "This couldn't be Thursday (note: this was their day of worship), I can still feel my feet;" and "Never trust a chief who paints his toenails;"

I share this example of Dunquat to demonstrate how difficult it can be to translate the spoken sound into written language. Since there are a limited number of human sounds that are broadly meaningful and acceptable in any culture, each sound can represent various objects or concepts. Therefore, the homonym. How the sound is used in context determines which agreed upon written spelling is to be used.

Back to the Ames Brothers song. When we hear them sing (phonetically,) "Ew, ew, ew," we cannot imagine they are singing either, "Ewe, ewe, ewe" about a female sheep, or, "Yew, yew, yew" about a beloved evergreen shrub in their yard. The challenge for all who function in a given language or dialect is to assume from the word's context in the spoken phrase what the written equivalent might be. That, in turn, assumes an established alphabet available in that language.

This brings me back to the overworked and under-appreciated letter *ω*. The "ooo" sound is one of the easiest for our mouth to produce. Therefore, that sound has long occupied an important first chair in the orchestra of the English language. As an advocate for the *ω*, I am a bit perturbed that this easy sound has so often been usurped by less deserving letters and combination of letters. *You, ewe,* and *yew* are examples of such usurpation.

First, the second person pronoun *you*. How did it come to be spelled in Modern English without my friend the *ω*? Over several hundred years, that was not always the case. One of the most common spellings in Old English of the pronoun was *eow* (probably pronounced something like "ee-o-oo"). The final vowel sound was represented with a *ω*. Curiously, our modern pronunciation of *you* is really quite similar. Some say "ee-u" while others get more sound, similar to Old English, with "ee-o-u." If we examine the incredible range of spellings of this word in Old English, it would seem clear that speakers at that time were getting this fuller sound. What's more, the *ω* is ubiquitous in this list: *ieow, iow, heou, heow, how, ou, hou, iou, æu, ew, heu, eo, oeu, howe, ow, owe, yew,* and *eu*. And, there were probably another dozen spelling variations. Have some fun and go back through this list, pronouncing each and listening for *ω*'s "ooo" sound.

To complicate things, in addition to these spellings using letters extant in our modern alphabet, many Old English spellings used the archaic letter *yogh* (ȝ), which was created by Norman scribes from the letter *g*.[29] The letter was sounded as the *s* in *vision*. Spellings using the *yogh* included: ȝeow, ȝuw, and ȝie. Try pronouncing those with your twenty-first century tongue! Possibly the two most common Middle English spellings for *you* were *eu* and ȝou.

Look again at that last Middle English spelling. Since the *y* and the ȝ were both in active use in Middle English, representing two different initial sounds in the second person pronoun, one can assume that our modern spelling of *you* may be the result of the easier pronunciation of the word nudging out the more difficult sound of "zh-o-u?"

I am disappointed that either the spelling *ew*, or even *eu*, did not win the evolutionary struggle for the sound of this word. That would certainly make it easier for our first-grade new readers to grasp the phonetics than does *you*. Some of you may not recall that moment of trauma when as a young child you mispronounced a simple reading word in front of the class. While doing a read-through of the script for a junior high play, I yet recall coming upon the French words, *oui* and *monsieur* in a phrase. I read the line, "Oo-eee (rhymes with *gooey*) mahnsewer, I would love to sample the pate (*paté*)." The joyful laughter of the director at my innocent mistake, not only embarrassed me in front of my friends, but has emotionally disfigured me for life. I still hold a deep, abiding dislike for the French. In my own neurotic way, I suspect *they* set this obvious trap for me by not spelling that word *oui* as *we*. It was the French who were responsible for me humiliating myself in front of my peers. I will have more to say about the French and their discomforting language later in my book.

But, we are all responsible for that youngster who encounters *you* for the first time and reads it aloud as "yee-oh-oo," like some street ruffian trying to get your attention on Fifth Ave.

with, "Yo, can you spare some of this money in your wallet?" Join with me in agreeing that from this day forward, we will spell the second person pronoun *ew*, for the sake of the children. If *ew* won't join me in this, the detrimental life consequences for our children will be on your head, not mine.

Go back now for a moment and notice that one of the Old English spellings for *you* was *yew*. I could live with that spelling. But, we have already glommed onto that spelling for some kind of evergreen. Old English had so many options available for that plant. Possibly the most common spelling for the plants from the Taxaceae family in Old English was *iuu*. Other spellings were: *iw* (see how much more user friendly the doubled *u* is here, compared to *iuu*?), *eow, eoh, ewe, ew, hw, hue, hew, uu, uv, u, eu, yeue, yue, ewgh, ugh, yeugh, eugh, yugh, yewgh, eue*, and even *yew*. *wOw*! Go back through *that* list and have fun pronouncing all those spellings. All pretty much sound the same, don't they? All could host a *w* easily, if given half a chance. Apparently the most common Middle English spelling of that word was *ew*, but for whatever reason the Printer Fates had in mind, *yew* eventually won (or *one*) out.

Here's a test for you, new student of the Double-U. If this spoken name for a plant had eventually been written simply as *w*, how would it/ should it have been pronounced? If your answer is "ooo," grab another cookie or chip from the bag (or whatever ew are eating right now) to celebrate your correct answer. But, that simple, easy-to-make sound was not what people were calling that plant. When people pointed at it, they did not call it an "ooo," they said it was an "ee-ooo." Since we have already agreed, from now till eternity, to use the spelling *ew* for the pronoun *you*, where does that leave us? We could return to the popular *iuu* Old English spelling. I think not! That seems an intentional attack on the viability of the *w*. May we just concur with linguistic history and accept the *yew* spelling? Seems agreeable, neat, and tidy to me. But, that still leaves this matter of using essentially the same sound for the second person pronoun, and for a Taxus, and also for a female sheep. What are we then to do with *ewe*? But first, let's consider what might seem to be an occasional, acceptable substitute for the *w*.

Are the Double-O and Double-U Sounds Interchangeable?

Some of the above discussion might lead one to think that the double-O in certain words represents the same sound as that characterized by our Beloved Double-U. Bite your tongue! The sound we are attempting to denote in such words as *wood*, *book*, and *look* is very close to the sound embodied in the letter Double-U, in such words as *two* (or *tw*), *throw*, or even *yew*. The subtle different in sound can be seen in the pronunciation guide in the front of your dictionary.

My best dictionary (we all have a few older, ratty ones on the shelf we just hate to throw away, don't we?) represents the *w as*" \w\ as in *w*e, and a*w*ay." Play with that sound a bit. For the double-o sound, the dictionary uses two different possibilities: "\u̇\, as in p*u*ll, w*oo*d, and b*oo*k." Try those a few times and see how that sound differs from the *w*. The other double-o sound can be seen in "u̇r, as in p*oo*r, t*ou*r, ins*ure*."[30] Give those a shot. Can you see the subtle difference between the three sounds? The *w* represents an "ooo" that is fully front in your lips. The other two sounds move back farther in the lips, toward the tongue. Phoneticians have names for all of these vowel positions. Why not call your local phonetician for a full list of vowel sound positions. You can find him/her in the *Yellow Pages* under, "People – Incredibly Boring."

Do I have a point to make in this boxed information.
Barely. I thought it was about time we broke away from my
long flow of exposition and boosted the excitement with
some text in a box. But, my point is, there are some sounds
we English-speaking people make that are quite close to
the sound represented by the *w*. But, those sounds are not
exactly the same, and they are represented on the page by
letters which are drab and unexciting. They do not have the
same sexy turn of ankle or curvaceous upsweeps as does
the bold and glamorous *w*. Hang out for awhile with some
oo's, some *ou's*, or even some *u's* and you will get my point.
They just don't bring much pizzazz to our mouth, or to the
page. If I'm teaching you anything, it is that the jealousy
harbored by many of the other letters in the English alphabet
has led them to imitate the *w*. Unfortunately, they have only
succeeded in embarrassing themselves on the printed page.
Oh, the phonetic vanity of letters which aspire to sounds not
suitable to their station!

Now, back to *ewe*. This is the third spelling for essentially the
same sound, with such disparate meanings. The list of various
Old English spellings seems to have been headed by *eowu*. This
would appear to indicate a slightly different articulation of the
name for a female sheep than what we have today. This gets a
bit of an *o* sound involved, in a word that matches our sound
for someone sticking his hand in scalding hot water: "ee-yow!"
The other spellings would raise the question of just what *was*
that female animal called: *awe, ouwe, ew, eawe, yoo, yeowe,
yew, ȝow, ȝoue*, and finally, *ewe*. By whatever path, this final
spelling has survived.

But wait! Notice the final *e* in the surviving spelling. And notice also the several other Old English spellings which included a final *e*. From Old English through Middle English, this final vowel would have been sounded, much as the final *e* in German words, as in *Goethe*. This means that when early English-speaking farmers pointed to this animal, they probably called it a "ee-ooo-uh." During that period of our language, it was apparently *not* a homonym for *you* and *yew*.

Once the Germanic influence on our language lost its ability to force us to sound the final *e*, it became a "ee-ooo." Consequently, I have a solution for the spelling of these three words, which will honor the *w* sound so prominent and proud in each:

- *You* should be spelled *ew*...no other Modern English word has that spelling.
- *Yew*, keep the spelling as *yew*
- *Ewe* should be spelled *ewa*, returning it to its proud pronunciation heritage.

This is a brief look at how simple it would be if we permitted the *w* her due. "Her" due? The *w* is feminine, rather than neuter? With curves like that, what do *you* think? I offer more on this suggestion that we should permit this powerful letter more frequency in print, thus improving the look and feel of written English. See Chapter Nine, "A Plea for Letter Economy: Words that *Should* Have a Double-U."

Chapter Sewen

Double-U and V: Centuries of Confusion

You may recall that I have encouraged my grandchildren to recite the close of our alphabet as, "….s, t, u, v, double-v, x, y, z." That is to alert the teacher that what she is trying to foist off on these impressionable minds is the letter *W*, which clearly is not a Double-U, but a double-v. We are the beneficiaries of centuries of confusion over these two letters. You and I should covenant that the confusion will end in our generation! Can we not finally call the *v* to account for attempting to gain some elegance and panache by mere close association with the *w* over these millennia?

How did this deception, this sham begin? How did we inherit a letter which combined two *v*'s into one letter and called it a Double-U? Who is to blame?

The history of the Double-U in Chapter Four made some mention of the confusing relationship between *v* and *w* over the centuries. It was noted that the *v* was among those letters which grew out of the Semitic letter *waw*, along with *f, u, w,* and y. In Greek the letter *upsilon* (*Y*) was adapted from *waw* to represent the vowel /u/ as in *moon*. In turn, Latin borrowed this Greek letter as a *v* (without the stem) to represent the same /u/ sound.[31]

The *v* became quite popular in the Latin language. It even served in Roman numerals as the number five. But it is most remember by English readers as a substitute for the letter *u* in such words as Jvlivs Caesar. One old saw was that this letter was used, rather than a *u*, since the straight line version was easier to carve into stone. That makes little sense when one observes how tricky the curved portions of *j*, *c*, and *s* were to carve. It is easier to believe that the Romans adapted the *upsilon*, as they did with so many aspects of Greek culture, to represent that same sound in Latin. Looks strange to us today because, through a lifetime of conditioning, we just can't bring ourselves to pronounce that *v* as a *u*! Try pronouncing that emperor's first name, as written above, with the v- sound. The English speaker cannot accomplish it without dislocating a lower lip.

With what did Latin represent the sound which we designate today with a *v*? That sound was handled by an *f*, much as it is in Modern German. The Ancient Latin small letter for this sound resembled a small, backward English *f*.

In the Medieval Period, two forms of the *u*, one with a rounded bottom and one that looked like our *v*, represented the *v*-sound. It wasn't until relatively modern times that the angular *v* was exclusively retained to presented our *v*-sound, and the version with the rounded bottom was left with the single job of representing the vowel *u*.[32] So, one can see that the perplexing interchangeability of these two letters has plagued us from ancient times.

Like the awkwardness between the *v* and the *u*, the Double-U spent a few centuries being viewed as a variant of the letter u, rather than a letter on its own. Its cause was helped by the arrival of printing in English in the 1470s. The Double-U shape was necessarily included with other metal letter blocks for printing English, and so its status as a separate letter became secure.[33]

The degree of difficulty is doubled when we get around to this introduction of the *w* to the mix. The *w* -sound, being distinctive from the *u*-sound, brings all three of these letters into a miasma of spoken and print fog. The Anglo-Saxons used a *v* for both the *u*- sound and the *v*-sound, and they wrote the *v* twice for the *w*-sound. Until the *w* had become firmly planted in our language, early printers used *vv* for lack of a *w* among their type. Yet, that coupling was required to be pronounced as a Double-U! To add yet another layer of difficulty to this confusion, the Germans eventually agreed upon the *v*-sound to be represented by the *w* in most of their words. That decision may have led to one of the great world conflicts in human history (see *The Real Cause of Vorld Var Tvoo* in the Addenda).

The French, for all time a thorn-in-the-flesh to English-speaking people, rather than use a foreign letter in their alphabet, preferred to double one of their own characters. They chose the *u* and called the letter "double vay." The English, once again needing to rectify the French, began calling it a "double-u."[34]

Given all this confusion between the *v* and the *w*, how then shall we live? Even the French got it half right! Can't we Anglos at least have the linguistic chutzpa to correct an outmoded, messy gaffe in our English alphabet? Can't we simply ban all typefaces, all fonts, which portray the Double-U as a W? That's all that I ask. Can't English-speaking people across the world make this simple correction, on behalf of the Majestic *w*? Doesn't that letter look so much more authoritative than a *W*?

w-lovers of the world unite! From this day forward, we shall not reproduce the W with any manual or electronic device at our disposal. We shall not read from any text which perpetuates this mockery. We shall call all publishers to task who contribute to this lazy, contemptible habit in print. Are you with me!? Please let me know how this works out for you, *w*ill ya?

MIDFACE

Midface? What's a Midface? It occurs to me that nearly every author begins his work with a Preface. Crammed into those opening thoughts are pretty much all the writer wants his reader to know about the volume to come. I tried that time-honored effort with this book. Problem is, now that I am about halfway through my writing plan, I've thought of all sorts of stuff I wish I had put into the Preface. Should I go back and deface the Preface? Not on your life! Therefore, voilá, the Midface. I invent this device for the use of all future authors who will follow my lead in rejecting the unwarranted constraints of the Preface.

* * * * *

First, **a special message** to all linguists, phoneticians, etymologists, and philologists who have read to this midpoint of my book. If you find my work simplistic, unprofessional, and poorly researched, please do me the honor of two things:

1. Re-read the Preface
2. Kiss off

* * * * *

You may have noticed my couple of derogatory remarks about the French earlier in the book. My *Preface* should have included the disclaimer that I am an unashamed Anglophile. Circumstances of birth and naming have left me little choice. With the surname White, I'm vetty English. The given name Wallace is so proudly Scottish. My middle name Whoolery must have been shouted across the moors in a number of English counties. Therefore, as a matter of heritage, I feel a certain obligation to insult the French.

Since my high school days, I have carried with me this bit of doggerel by G.K. Chesterton. It has long served as my call-to-arms:

> *Oh, how I love Humanity*
> *With love so pure and pringlish,*
> *And how I hate the horrid French,*
> *Who never will be English!*

I have paid a bit of tribute to my love for the English with the title for this book. By using the British spelling of "defence," I have done at least two things. One, I honor those who provided us Americans with our rich, complex, fascinating language. Two, and I have waited until this far along in my book to bring this up, I have allowed you to wonder if I just don't know how to spell "defense." *That* I know how to spell. But, I am still a bit perplexed about that *judgement* or *judgment* thing.

What is my immediate quandary with the French? It's their lack of embarrassment in perpetuating a written language which bears such phony relationship to their spoken language. The French speak one way, yet foist a written language on the world which bears so little resemblance to what they are saying. They have conspired against the outside world to make us all look like fools when we try to pronounce their written language. By that I mean, all those final consonants which they insist on using but have no bloody intention of pronouncing!

Heaven forbid that in Paris one should order a *chocolat* ("sho-ko-lah") and sound the final *t* ("sho-ko-laht"). Or that we would say *please* by sounding the final *t* in *s'il vous plait*, as "seel-voo-plate." The French have deliberately chosen to make all non-French speaking people look like twits when we try to speak their language! They have agreed to pepper their written words with final consonants which they agree not to pronounce, but snigger among themselves when we fall into the trap of pronouncing them.

A timely example is my own embarrassment at the hands of the conniving French language *gendarmes*. A few years ago an incredible French Canadian troupe began mesmerizing world audiences. They chose the enchanting name *Cirque du Soleil*, the "Circus of the Sun." As I encountered that intriguing name for the first time, a rule from my college French class came immediately to mind. The principle is that you do not pronounce a final consonant except for those consonants found in the word CAREFUL. Therefore, *soleil* ends with an *l*, and there is an *l* in CAREFUL, so the word must be pronounced "so-lay-eel." I went around for months singing the group's praises and calling them the "Sir-k doo so-lay-eel." How mortified I was when the teen girl's voice on the other end of the drive-thru speaker at McDonalds corrected me with, "I'm sorry, sir, but that should be pronounced "Sir-k doo so-lay!" Just one more mark in my diary of embarrassing moments caused by the French.

Of course the French-speakers will defend themselves by noting that they do permit the sounding of these final consonants if they are followed by a word beginning with a vowel. I am permitted to sound the final *t* if I am saying, *"Puis-je obtenir un chocolat au Cirque du Soleil"* ("Can I get a chocolate at the Cirque du Soleil?"). Sorry, too little too late. If the only way I can sound the *t* here is to go to the stupid circus, I will simply forgo that sweet, pleasurable, irresistible caffeine boost.

Here's the point I want you fragile Francophiles to get. If human language is first spoken, then written, what could possibly be the explanation (or the justification) for the French language? It appears that most human societies who set out to craft a written language attempt to create an alphabet consisting of letters which can generally represent the oral sounds already present in their spoken language. But, no, not the French. They have run around smugly speaking one of the most beautiful languages ever mouthed, but turned nasty when setting it to alphabet. They have just stuck onto the ends of their words, in an apparently willy-nilly fashion, consonants which do not represent the sounds they have been making. What could a people's motive possibly be in doing such a thing, if it were not to simply embarrass those who try to learn their language? Few people know this is an ancient conspiracy. I can now reveal that this conspiracy is known to us serious professionals in the linguistics business as *"Code Secret Françaises"* (French Secret Code). The code is revealed to no one who is not comfortable wearing a beret.

But there is an additional deep, dark secret known only to the cabal that has long managed this secret intrigue. The French are responsible for an international black market trade in surplus consonants! The dubious dealings of this clandestine agency known by some as *Les Négociants en Consonnes*, (The Traders in Consonants) have operated for centuries just a mere thirty miles from the coast of our beloved England. Their intrigue can now be revealed!

My research has uncovered a direct link between *Les Négociants* in France and the creation of the Polish language.

The agency has been gathering and shipping to Poland the leftover, unused consonants at the end of French words for centuries. Estimates of the volume of trade in these clandestine consonants in just the tenth century (the time of the birthing of Polish) was upwards of twenty-seven thousand consonants! Most shipments in those early years appear to have included a disproportionate number of *Z's*.

Prior to those transfers of surplus consonants from Paris to Warsaw, the Polish language had consisted primarily of lose combinations of vowels and accent marks. Though the trade payments back to Paris were a heavy burden (consisting mostly of a combination of sausages, other processed pork fat, and water bagels), the dependable source of consonants would transform the map of Poland. A list of city names in 1058 shows the sad dearth of consonants in early Poland. Next are the names of those cities today, bolstered by the black market French consonants, with today's approximate population.

City name c1058	City Name Today	Population
Ocla	Wroclaw	400,000
Ecin	Szczecin	200,000
Ol	Olsztyn	20,000
Ów	Rzeszów	18,000

One can see what riches the French consonant trade has meant to Poland. But at what cost to both France and Poland? The French are left with a language which is about as user-friendly as a do-it-yourself home appendectomy kit. Further, they have racked up a continuing, embarrassing trade deficit with Poland, leaving most French households with a daily portion of more Kielbasa and bagels than any family can eat in a month. And the Poles? They have now run a consonant surplus for one hundred-fifty consecutive years. This has led to one new suburb of Kraków, Poland's second largest city, having to accept the name *Zlskrychskz*. Yes, Poland is now running out of vowels. At whose doorstep may we place this tragic state of affairs? The thoughtless French, of course![35]

Chapter Eight

Double and Triple-U's

Now that I have that off my chest, let's try to move on. I can sense some lingering outrage toward the French in some of you readers, but we must continue building our defence of the foremost letter in the English alphabet. The growing evidence of the *w*'s supremacy leads us now to consider yet another versatility of the letter. It's mere existence combines two letters into one. Now I propose to demonstrate that, much like today's figure skaters, our friend the *w* can even occasionally sustain a triple.

I mentioned earlier that there are few words in the English language which have a *w* followed by a *u*. This would, in fact, create a triple *u*, a nearly unimaginable feat for any consonant or vowel. My humble dictionary records these unusual triple feats:

- wu – a group of Chinese dialects
- wud – a descendent of the Middle English word *wude* (wood), a slang term used mostly by the Scottish to mean "mad or insane"
- Wulfenite – a mineral named for an Austrian mineralogist

- wunderkind – a word for a child prodigy, borrowed directly from the German
- wurst – again a word direct from the German, meaning "sausage"
- wushu – a Chinese martial art, the word coming straight from Chinese
- wuss – a slang term for a wimp (origin unknown)
- wuther – a genuine English word meaning "to blow with a dull, roaring sound"

A quick review of this list will show only two triple-u words coming to us from the English: *wud* and *wuther*. The first is not in general English usage. The second, however, has lived on, thanks to Emily Bronte's beloved novel *Wuthering Heights*.
There is probably a tendency among uninformed readers to pronounce her title "Withering Heights," due to a lack of familiarity with the actual word. Bronte's title has captured not only the dull, roaring sound of the wind across the Yorkshire moors, but has kept alive the only true English-source triple-*u* word in modern English usage. If you are skeptical about this fascinating linguistics claim, look it up in your Funk & Wagnalls.

Such a claim could not be made by those speaking/writing Middle English, however. Our ancestors employed many more triples:

- wuch – for *which*
- wude – *wood* or *tree*
- wule – *while*, also *will*
- wundi – *rid of*
- wune – *accustomed*
- wunien – *to dwell*

- wunne – *joy*
- wurne – *to refuse*
- wurse – *worse*
- wuschen – *to wish*
- wute – *know*

The power of position assigned the *w* over the centuries has led to essentially all *u*'s which have followed immediately after an initial *w* being changed to another vowel. Examples above are wuch/which, wude/wood, wule/while, and wurse/worse. Does this argue one way or the other for the *w* as either a consonant or a vowel? May I suggest that if the *w* were considered a consonant in any of these words, why the problem with a vowel following a simple consonant, eh? The tripling of the same vowel in English words is quite rare. I submit that this triple-*u* etymology would argue in favor of the *w* being seen as a double vowel in these words.

This leaves us, however, with another thorny problem with our growing assumption of the power and prestige of the *w*. There remains some words in English which still have a double–*u* vowel combination which have not been combined into a Double-U! How could this be? Who was asleep at the linguistics switch when these malformed words were permitted to move out of the word yard onto the track of Modern English?

I give you these twisted, deformed, English words which have escaped the normal evolutionary process, and the sordid history of each:

- continuum – Borrowed directly from the Latin as a form of *continuus*, the meaning of which also carries over to the English. As can be seen in my history of the *w*, classic Latin did not have such a letter choice in its alphabet. Some might suggest this was just one more reason for the fall of the Roman Empire.

- duumvir – Also directly from the Latin, the word meant either member of a two-person governing board (with the same meaning today).

- menstruum – Again an awkward gift from Latin. Our word means a solvent which can dissolve and hold a solid. Ours is a form of the Latin *menstrual*, one form of the Latin for *month*.

- muumuu – A nearly English word, since it was borrowed from the native Hawaiian language. Everyone who was around in the '60's remembers this as a loose-fitting dress. Though the Hawaiian alphabet does have both a *u* and a *w*, it is not unusual in that written language of just 12 letters (five vowels and seven consonants) to use a doubled *u* to represent our *w* sound.

- residuum –Yet again, directly from the Latin. Our word *residue* comes from this root word which means something left over, especially from some kind of process. A surprising amount of our English language is residuum from the struggles our language had being birthed, in large part, from Latin.

- triduum – Can you guess the source? Right. This Latin word means "three days," and is used most often today in the Christian church for a three-day period of prayer. Are you seeing a clear pattern developing here?

- vacuum – Finally a word in most of our active vocabularies. But, were you aware that, once again, we've borrowed this directly from the Latin (meaning "empty space")? The Latin *vacuus* also means "empty."

Notice that given enough time to deal with that spelling, in English we have gotten rid of that double-*u* awkwardness with our English spelling *vacuous*. We can only tolerate that strange double vowel form for so long before we make it right for *ɯ*-Lovers everywhere. If the Catholic church can move away from the strictures of Latin, cannot we outside the nave do the same?

- weltanschauung – Here's one we can't blame on Latin. This direct transfer from German is from *welt* (world) and *anschauung* (view), making its meaning "a worldview" or comprehensive concept. I'll just need to let this one pass. Centuries of history have shown us that there is no reason to even try to bring order or reason to the Germans and their language. Make them mad and they will just stick several more words on the end of *weltanschauung* and no one on Earth would be able to pronounce it. After all this time, if they haven't even given in to the broad world's pronunciation of *ɯ*, what luck are we going to have in trying to clean up an occasional *uu* in their Germanic weltanschauung?

Well, there you have it. Eight words commonly used in English which have not had their primitive coupling of two *u*'s surgically corrected with a *ɯ* transplant. Today we correct that malady. How would those words look corrected? See if you are able to easily pronounce these corrected spellings, using the new embouchure you have developed for sounding the *ɯ*:

- continwm
- dwmvir
- menstrwm
- mwmw

- residwm
- tridwm
- vacwm
- weltanschawng (This one may actually damage your embouchure, so be careful here.)

Any problems? You're actually getting pretty good at this. Can't we stand together and agree to ask all those within our sphere of influence to adopt these spellings? This would clean up the few remaining loose ends in what we might call the *w* Conversion Mission. We are getting close to our goal, so we must agree not to ~~uuaver~~ waver.

Chapter Nine

A Plea for Letter Economy: Words Which Should Have a *W*

Each letter of our alphabet has an essence of its own. Each an intrinsic, distinctive feel and sound of its own. These unique letter characteristics have become part of our mostly unspoken, habitual culture.

Some letters are harsh: *p*, *q*, *t*. Pronounce those sounds out loud. On their own, those letters are just hard and severe. They either explode through our lips or teeth, or they gargle in the back of our throat. There is no way we can soften those letters, except by bringing a softer letter to their defense: phone, quiet, though. These letters can only achieve sociability with a little help from their friends.

Some letters are apparently funny, in and of themselves. In Neil Simon's play *The Sunshine Boys*, the aging comedy partner Willy (played in the movie by Walter Matthau) explains to his nephew, "Words with a *k* in them are funny. *Alka-Seltzer* is funny. *Chicken* is funny. *Pickle* is funny. All with a *k*. *L*'s are not funny. *M*'s are not funny."

The intrinsic feel and meaning of certain letters are especially felt when they are tripled. Do you sense an action or mood when you see *zzz* or *sss*? The first is sleep and the latter is hot…something like the sizzle of a steak or the sound of steam.

What have you found so far to be the essence of *w*? This will be on the final, so you should best have it right by now. There is an innate feel of pleasure, calm, even joy in the *w*. Therefore it is chosen for words like *wow!*, and *whew!* If you have learned to pronounce the letter correctly, you should now be able to ignore the inaccurate font and pronounce this triple: *www!*. Give it a try. The sound should be "ooo." How soothing, how cooling, how calming, but how confusing to the uninitiated. If you got it right, you may skip the final.

A premise of this book is that the letter *w* is so much more, has so much more potential, than the history of our language, and today's practitioners of English, are willing to allow her. I hope by this point you are beginning to allow some of that premise. If you are, this next exercise should be fun for you. If you are still unconvinced, you may want to skip this exercise and return for a time to TV game shows or admiring the sweet, subtle sounds of French, until Chapter Ten.

Now that we have weeded out a few more skeptics, you and I can enjoy the following. For the sake of letter economy for all English speaking nations (but especially for those of us speaking American English) I would suggest the following spellings for a number of common English words. Pronounce the word using your best *w* sound. Then, write in the blank provided the current, awkward, extravagant spelling of that sound. In the second blank, note the number of vowel savings for this smarter spelling.

With this exercise, I am also inaugurating a new international relief program to help offset the damage done to the Polish language over the centuries by the French. The *Vowel Relief Project for Poland* (V.R.P.P.) will begin gathering all these vowels saved by using the more efficient *w* spellings. We will then make regular shipments to our relief workers living in Warsaw. These much needed vowels will then be distributed to newspapers and book publishers across Poland.

The correct answers for this exercise may be found in the Addenda. Once you have identified the number of surplus vowels from your exercise page, you are asked to please transfer those letters onto quality, recycled paper and send your donations to: The Vowel Relief Project for Poland, 1297 Casimir Polasky Hwy., Archer Heights, IL 12345. No e-mailed donations please. The linguistics terror group *Les Négociants* of France regularly hack our V.R.P.P. website and are redirecting the lists to a vowel black market ring operating out of Nigeria.[36]

(***Author's note***: anyone who regularly generates text messages might want to copy this chapter to whatever electronic device supports your lonely, nervous habit.)

English Words Which Should Be Spelled with a *ɯ*

<u>Recommended Spelling</u> / <u>Current, Awkward Spelling</u> / (<u>No. of Vowels Saved</u>)

adw / _____ / ()	lws / _____ / ()	spwn / _____ / ()
bwth / _____ / ()	lwp / _____ / ()	swn / _____ / ()
cw / _____ / ()	lwvr / _____ / ()	swt / _____ / ()
cwp / _____ / ()	mwr / _____ / ()	swvenir/ _____ / ()
cwth / _____ / ()	mws / _____ / ()	tw / _____ / ()
ew / _____ / ()	mwt / _____ / ()	twl / _____ / ()
fwd / _____ / ()	mwv / _____ / ()	twt / _____ / ()
flw / _____ / ()	nw / _____ / ()	twth / _____ / ()
grwv / _____ / ()	nwn / _____ / ()	twcan / _____ / ()
gwrmet/ _____ / ()	nwrish / _____ / ()	wz / _____ / ()
gws / _____ / ()	pwr / _____ / ()	wlong / _____ / ()
hwray / _____ / ()	pwf / _____ / ()	wol / _____ / ()
jwse / _____ / ()	pwl / _____ / ()	wwzy / _____ / ()
jwl / _____ / ()	rwl / _____ / ()	ywth / _____ / ()
kwak / _____ / ()	rwm / _____ / ()	zw / _____ / ()
kwik / _____ / ()	rwt / _____ / ()	zwt swt/ _____ / ()
kwk / _____ / ()	rwlet / _____ / ()	
lwz / _____ / ()	skwl / _____ / ()	Total vowels saved ____

Chapter Ten

The Double-U in Other Languages

Human communication is first oral, then communal, then written. Human creative genius includes our innate drive to point at an object (or person) and call it something. It did not seem to be enough that our primitive forebears could look, admire, then walk way fulfilled. We appear to have an inherent need to produce some sort of sound with which that object or person can be identified in the future.

Add to this the near infinite variety and range of sounds the human voice can produce. Ingo R. Titze, a world leader in the scientific study of the human voice, writes, "Although the human vocal system is small, it manages to create sounds as varied and beautiful as those produced by a variety of musical instruments. The human voice can create such an impressive array of sounds because it relies on nonlinear effects, in which small inputs yield surprisingly large outputs."[37] This should give us a picture of generations of people over the millennia across the globe pointing and creating naming sounds for everything that moves or stands in place.

This inborn tendency for humankind to assign names to everything in sight is reflected in the Hebrew Bible's book of Genesis, "the book of beginnings." In the second creation account in that book, after Yahweh (notice our transliteration of this supreme name even contains a *w*) had finished creating "Every animal of the field and every bird of the air," He paraded them past the first human to see "What he would call them." Part of the original human fiber seems to be that we are not content until everything around us has a name, some sort of word assigned to it.

That reminds me of the story of the baseball game where the ball hits the catcher's glove and the umpire delays a bit before calling it a ball or a strike. The catcher looks back at the ump and says, "Come on ump, is it a ball or a strike!?" He replied calmly, "It's nothing, until I call it something." Small, daily aspects of human reality do not seem complete until everything in our sight has been named. Look around you right now. Can't you name everything within sight, regardless of where you find yourself at the moment? Don't we find great comfort in knowing what to call something? Aren't we even relieved when the doctor finally assigns a name to the cause of our symptoms?

In primitive societies the problem then arises when various members of the tribe make different sounds for the same object or person. A young man in a remote village along the Amazon discovers a large piece of Styrofoam which has washed up on the bank of the river. Having never seen such a strange substance before, he calls it "lolu," meaning *new*. He takes it back to his village and shows it to his father. Dad examines it, throws it into the air, and pronounces it shall be called "tahko," meaning *light*. Dad takes it to the tribal chief, who breaks off a piece, tastes it, spits it out, and declares it is to be known as "fahnua," meaning *inedible*. Some sort of agreement must be reached as to *which* word will be the acceptable one for that group of people. There is no problem figuring out which of these three words becomes standard vocabulary for that tribe. The chief is right, whatever he might call it. But, how does that tribe provide some sort of written record of the winning word for future members of the tribe?

A much later step in the development of all of our languages is the stage in which the growing, dispersing tribe desires to communicate beyond earshot. This desire may be to both reach those not immediately at hand and to leave some sort of message for those in future generations. This must have created a gigantic hurdle for most civilizations. We've already speculated that one group has usually silenced the weaker members of the tribe. The next task is finding people in the tribe who like to make scratches on stone or paper. Probably all of you reading this book will certainly know that you would have been the withdrawn, lonely types who would have been the most likely ones chosen to sit around and write stuff down. Someone has to come forward to begin the process of transcribing these consensus sounds into some sort of written language. This phase in human language development apparently begins with attempts at written symbols to stand for specific human sounds. Thus, the alphabet.

Early pictograms required writers and readers to memorize hundreds of specific images representing words and ideas. Some Asian alphabets still have that demanding requirement. Later alphabets though were a kind of phonetic shorthand in which many basic sounds could be strung together to form words.

Most modern alphabets can trace their lineage back as far as the Middle Bronze Age (2000-1500 B.C.). The early hieroglyphs served as picture symbols for objects and persons. My Chapter Four provides some brief notes on the development of systems of symbols which eventually led to the adoption of letters. The earliest system of letter symbols which we might recognize as an alphabet would date to the civilization from which our English world *alphabet* comes: the Greeks. The word itself is a combination of the first two letters of the Greek alphabet, *alpha* and *beta*.

An alphabet is simply a list of those letter symbols available to be used by writers of that language, singly or in unlimited combinations, to represent the various sound combinations upon which a people group has agreed. The first of such letter lists with which English writers would be reasonably comfortable would be Classical Latin, which led to the Roman alphabet. That latter list included all our twenty-six English letters. The Roman alphabet serves as a basis for writing most of the languages of Western Europe.

So what does this brief trip back to early human grunts and whistles have to do with my beloved *w*? The mere fact the letter might appear in the alphabet of a language other than English does not ensure that it will represent the same human vocal we assign her in our language. I have suggested that the sound the *w* characterizes in English is the beautiful "ooo" vocal. It is that gentle, loving, open sound we make when we encounter a lovely sight. When we watch fireworks or glimpse a beautiful sunset, we might say "o-o-o." When we make that sound our lips are protruding a bit, the air flow is open, almost as in preparation for a kiss. That's it! The *w* is our most romantic letter. It is the strawberries and chocolate of letters. Who could resist such a sound?

In the midst of an infinite variety of human vocalizations, the "ooo" sound may or may not even be included in a given oral language tradition. Specific languages are even recognizable by certain vocal tendencies. I'm sure your ear can recognize the range of guttural utterances in German, or the amazing inflection ranges of several Asian tongues, or even the gentle, self-effacing sounds of French (a painful admission for me). But, most Western languages have at least a passive relationship with the *w*, even if they choose it to represent a sound different than our passionate pucker in English. Let's examine the place of my friend the *w* in a few other Western languages.

There are only five major European languages which use *w* in native words: English, German, Polish, Dutch, and Welsh. Let's start with German. It provides the most obvious conflicts with our English concept of the *w* (see Chapter Sewen). Then, following the other four, we'll take a look at a few other foreign languages' uses of the letter.

- **German** – The German letter *w* ("vay") is pronounced in most words like an English *v*. Many of us encountered this difference when the German car Volkswagen first came to our shores. It presented a quick education in the German sound because the name had both a *v* and a *w* in the same word. Those of us in the know paraded our "Volks-vahgen" pronunciation before our friends, feigning some heretofore unknown Continental experiences. The correct pronunciation didn't seem to catch on, though, since most Americans have continued to say "Volks-wagon." The *w* in German is pronounced as *v* even in clusters with other consonants, such as in *Schweiz* (Switzerland), *zwei* (two....or tvoo), and *Schweden* (Sweden). Another difference from English is that a German *w* is sounded in *wr* combinations, as in *wrack* (wreck) and *wringen* (to write). The *w* in English may or may not be silent in this combination (see Chapter Three).

- **Polish** – The Polish alphabet includes the *w* (a letter called "wu"), but it is pronounced the same as it is in German. One difference is that our sound for *w* is covered in Polish by the letter Ł.

- **Dutch** – The letter *w* in Dutch is *wé* (pronounced "way"). Unlike their German and Polish neighbors, the Dutch have distinct *v* and *w* sounds. The *w* is sounded as in English. Their letter *u* serves a bit more of the *y* sound heard in English. Dutch even includes an *uw* diphthong which sounds a bit like our *ew* ("ee-oo") pronunciation. A sprint through a Dutch dictionary will reveal many similarities to other Germanic languages, with the exception of the wisdom the Dutch have had in celebrating the glorious, full-lipped sound of our favorite letter. *Dank u, Nederlands!*

- **Spanish** – In the second most common language in our nation, the *w* is called by several names: *doble ve, ve doble, doble u* or *doble uve*. It is used almost exclusively in words of foreign origin. Some listings of the Spanish alphabet do not include the *w*. A quick scan of any Spanish dictionary will reveal precious few *w* words.

- **French** – This is a language where the sound represented in English by *w* is rather common, but our letter is seldom used for that "ooo" sound. The French alphabet does include the *w*, but its use (along with the letter *k*) is limited almost exclusively to words borrowed from other languages. The French *w* is known as *double vé* ("doo-bluh vay"). The vowel combination most often used for our *w* sound is *ou*. We just saw that in play in the French pronunciation of *double*. The vowel combination there is our friend the "ooo." The language that brought us "Oo-la-la" should reconsider more use of the *w*. It could provide them with a fresh, renewed level of romance. It might improve their attitude toward English-speaking people as well.

- **Italian** – Once again we have a language known for its potential for deep expressions of *amore*, yet it lacks the love power of the *w*. The Italian alphabet is a variant of the older Latin alphabet. It consists of 21 letters, not including a *w* (nor a *j*, *k*, *x*, or *y*). When used in words from foreign languages, the Italian *w* is known as *doppia vu*. Our *w* sound is normally represented in Italian by the *u*. If they only knew they could *doppia* their pleasure!

- **Portuguese** – This Romance Language does include our romantic letter in its alphabet. The *w* is known by any of three names: dábliu, dáblio, or duplo-vê. In both the Portuguese of Portugal and of Brazil, the letter can represent either a *v* or an "ooo" sound. Once again, as with the Romance Languages Spanish, French, and Italian, the *w* (also *k* and *y*) are used only in foreign-loaned words.

- **Swedish** – The dynamic, ever evolving nature of language can be seen in the history of the *w* in Swedish. The Swedish alphabet uses the 26 letters of the Latin alphabet, plus three others (two variations of the *a* and one of the *o*). Again, words in Swedish using a *w* are foreign words. *w* and *v* are pronounced identically in Swedish ("vee"), and therefore the letters have been considered interchangeable. Until recently the letter *w* was treated as a variant form of *v*, at least for sorting purposes, and this practice is still commonly encountered. However, in 2005 the Swedish Academy separated the two letters in conformity with international lexicographic practice.[38] This means that words spelled with the rarer *w* have been listed under the "V" section of the dictionary. Since 2005, the new version of the Swedish Academy's dictionary now has a section for *w*, all by itself. To that I say, "*Tack, Sverige!*" ("Thank you, Sweden!").

Chapter Elewen

The Other WWW

Is there one triple letter combination that is recognized in nations throughout the world? A combination of three alliterative letters which is recognizable to readers of any language on the globe?

Could it be AAA, the American Automobile Association? These initials are certainly known by most Americans, but not much beyond our shores. How about BBB, the Better Business Bureau? About the only people outside commerce who know this combination are those Americans who have a complaint because some sleazy contractor has installed their replacement roofing with thumb tacks, then skipped town. Then maybe CCC? The Civilian Conservation Corp is still remembered by some who survived the Great Depression, but that New Deal program to rebuild America's infrastructure has not cut a hiking trail through the woods since its demise in 1942. It was never well known beyond American woods. Ah, but how about KKK? Surely these initials still stir a certain amount of panic in the hearts of peace-loving people everywhere? Not so much. The Ku Klux Klan is a bit of a toothless tiger. The mostly White Supremacy group these days provides more comic relief than terror on the evening news. They stand as a popgun among the cannons of international terrorist groups, and were only active in America's Lower 48. Then surely the infamous XXX designation demands attention around the world, wherever it is attached to truly hardcore pornography? Again, not so much. The Motion Picture Association of America (America being the operative word here) originally used an X-rating designation for movies suitable only for adults. Creative purveyors of porno upped the ante with their unofficial XXX-rating for movies aimed primarily at men on whom Viagra was beginning to lose its potency. Though this might have been the most famous triple-letter designation in the world prior to 1990, the year the World Wide Web was established, it quickly faded when home delivery of porno through the family computer made movie ratings pretty much moot.

WWW, of course! The World Wide Web is the most recognizable triple-letter combination in the entire universe. That, lacking any evidence that Wi-Fi definitely cannot reach beyond our atmosphere. The W.W.W. rules!!

I was *www* long before Al Gore began inventing the Internet. I like to think the World Wide Web is actually my name sake. As a young man, though, I did not have the foresight to register my initials. I could have made a killing. Too late now, so I will just bask in the light of the world's most famous initials. If any of you readers also share mine and the WWW's triple *w* initials, give me a call. Even at this late date, I suspect we might be able to persuade an attorney somewhere to launch some sort of class action suit on our behalf.

Were you aware that I am blocked from the Internet from using my three initials as a domain name? Try www.www.com and see what you get. Now try www.www.org. There is no such animal there, either! It comes up www.w3.org, which is the website for the World Wide Web Consortium. Don't you think I have grounds for a suit here? Even though no one else has been assigned the www.com domain name, apparently those of us wanting to represent our proud initials are blocked, just because it somehow throws the great World Wide Web group in some sort of hissy fit. Do you now see the power imbued in those of us with my three initials? We can intimidate the international cartel (whoever and wherever they are) that runs the Internet!

This is yet one more proof that the *w* is the most impressive letter in the English alphabet. Developers of the World Wide Web could have chosen other names and alliterative initial combinations to entice users into their international web of intrigue and deceit. In those early days of meager information offerings they might have chosen NNN for the "Nattering Nabob Net." Or, maybe ZZZ for "Zonked Zed Zone." Or how about OOO for "Only Online Occasionally?" But the fact is, those computer pioneers must have seen the attention grabbing power they could generate by grouping three of the widest letter in nearly every type font: the *w*. Turns out, WWW is also the longest possible three-letter acronym to pronounce, requiring nine syllables: "double-u, double-u, double-u." Whereas, the twelve letters in "World Wide Web" are pronounced with only three syllables. There's power and mystery in the *w*! Pronounce *wwww* backwards and you get "u-elbuod, u-elbuod, u-elbuod."? Strangely enough, this is the exact sound of the question most often shouted by straphangers on the NYC subway ("Who elbowed, who elbowed, who elbowed!?"). One just can't overlook these kinds of peculiar coincidences when it comes to the ancient hidden mysteries of the *w*.

Note to reader: Listen carefully to how you are pronouncing the *www* in web addresses. If after all you've learned here you are still saying "Dubya, dubya, dubya," please schedule yourself a 24-hour fast sometime this week as your proper penance. Meditate and reflect deeply on the encumbrance you continue to load upon the back of the assiduous *w*. Ask yourself, "Would I be so insensitive to other letters?"

The previous chapter gave details on the occurrence and pronunciation of *w* in several Western languages. One can see from that brief discussion that the www initials in the beginning of all World Wide Web websites causes a bit of problem for speakers of many languages other than English. This is particularly true of those languages which contain no *w* in their alphabet.

Computer users around the world must bow to the *w*. They have no choice but to include the www, as strange as those letters might seem to them, in their daily discourse. Can you imagine how peculiar and frustrating it might be for all us English-speaking Internet addicts to encounter long lists of domain names which all began with жжж, the letter zh ("zheh") in the Russian alphabet? Imagine our encountering a website address such as жжж.funwithfudge.com? How would we pronounce the first part of that address? This strange looking combination can give us the sense of what many foreign-speaking Internet users experience every day. Whether or not they know what a *w* is, they must accommodate it every time they log on.

For those readers who do not regularly connect with foreign language websites, the standard format is: *www*, followed by the domain name in the language of the nation, followed by appropriate suffixes, then the country code. An example in French: www.lequipe.fr (a site for team sports news). Regardless of the language, then, the *www* is a given universal in the address.

Now, aren't you grateful that you have this long, loving relationship with our favorite letter? We find nothing to trip us up, regardless of the web address. Our friend the Double-U leads the way in all addresses, regardless of the nation of origin.

And our ability to pronounce the first part of Web addresses is comfortable and easy: "Double-u, double-u, double-u dot…. something and something." Pronouncing this triple initial by speakers of many other languages, though, becomes problematic. How do they speak those three initials when they wish to orally provide their website address to others? Certainly not with the casual ease with which you and I *w*-Lovers do.

A *Wikipedia* article lists pronunciations for the opening letters of a few foreign language websites[39]. Here are the ways a few non-English speaking people refer to the first part of their website addresses:

Czech - "vé, vé, vé" (pronounced "vay-vay-vay")

Dutch – "wé, wé, wé" ("way-way-way")

Estonian – "vee, vee, vee" (pronounced as appears)
> Note: This is also the common pronunciation in Finnish, Norwegian, Swedish and Danish.)

Finnish – The longer version is "kaksoisvee, kaksoisvee, kaksoisvee" (see above)

French – "double vé, double vé, double vé" ("doo-bluh vay")

Icelandic – "tvöfalt vaff, tvövalt vaff, tvöfalt vaff" (or, usually just "vaff, vaff, vaff," the pronunciation of the Icelandic letter for *v*)

Italian – "doppia vu, doppia vu, doppia vu" (pronounced as it looks)

Hungarian – "duplavé, duplavé, duplavé" (or more often, same as Czech)

Macedonian (and Serbian) - "ве, ве, ве" ("vee-vee-vee")

Polish – "wu, wu, wu" ("voo-voo-voo")

Portuguese (Portugal) – "dablio, dablio, dablio" (pronounced as it looks)

Russian – "вэ, вэ, вэ" ("vee-vee-vee")

Spanish – (many options here) "doble u, doble u, doble u,"
"doble ve, doble ve, doble ve," "uve doble, uve doble,
uve doble," "triple doble u," "triple doble ve," or "triple
uve doble"

Turkish – "dabıl yu, dabıl yu, dabıl yu" or "çift ve, çift ve,
çift ve" (or simply "ve, ve, ve")

This list points up the worldwide power of *w*. People around
the world have had to adapt their daily lives to accommodate
this internationally authoritative letter of the English alphabet.
Makes me proud of my namesake. The World Wide Web has
done all of us proud, all of us who bear the regal initials *w.w.w.*
If I were ever to have another daughter, I am certain I would
name her "Dot Com White," just to continue this proud family
tradition.

Ah, but lest we forget, 'twas not I who actually began the
triple- *w* lineage. That was initiated exactly a century before
my birth, in 1841. Scottish poet William Miller created the
proud progenitor of all of us who carry the brand *w*³. In that
year he gave birth to *Wee Willie Winkie*. In Scottish he wrote:

Wee Willie Winkie rins through the toun,
Up stairs and doon stairs in his nicht-goun,
Tirlin' at the window, cryin' at the lock,
"Are the weans in their bed, for it's noo ten o'clock?"

We have made it a bit less tuneful in common English:

Wee Willie Winkie
Runs through the town,
Upstairs and downstairs
In his nightgown.

Rapping at the windows,
Crying through the lock,
"Are the children all in bed,
For it's now ten o'clock?"

I struggled for many weeks over the dedication of this book. It rightfully should have been dedicated to *Wee Willie Winkie*, my most beloved benefactor. At the last moment, however, my heart turned to "Willard the Wonder Weasel," a cartoon character my three children and I proposed many years ago. Poor Willard never felt the tickle of the cartoonist's pen. There apparently was not room amid the avalanche of cartoon drivel on Saturday mornings for a gangly super-hero rodent with a winsome smile and a body of steel. Alas, hapless Willard died aborning. It is to his memory, my three creative offspring and I dedicate this book. Willard, we hardly knew ye.

Chapter 12

What Other Letters Deserve an Apologist?

I hope I have made my case convincingly enough to you that you have found a new respect and love for the much maligned letter Double-U. A healthier *w* in American society could usher in a time of broader justice and compassion for all our citizens. I see such an era as an age of a stronger economy and more widespread love and charity to the poor and downtrodden. Your new understanding of the power of the *w* could help reshape America's societal priorities, leading to a new dawn.

I am not such a Dublophile, however, that I am unable to see centuries of unwarranted and vicious neglect of at least two other letters in the English alphabet. I would be remiss if my sense of fairness, even my magnanimity, did not cry out for someone to defend these two letters as well. Surely among you readers there is at least one with the initials R.R.R. who has seen throughout your years the injustices foisted on your letter! Will you not stand up today and accept the challenge to correct the slights and point up the careless neglect of the English-speaking world toward your letter? Lest you have been blinded also, to these centuries of assault, let me help you gather your resolve. If you are a Ronald Raoul Reynolds or a Ryan Ragland Ross, won't you answer this call?

In addition, certainly one of you more gentle readers, who has borne the life-long yoke of the initials Y.Y.Y., could be persuaded to finally come to your letter's defense. Haven't you noticed that our English culture has taken for granted this soft, unassuming letter? We have relegated it to confused, second-class letter status, not unlike my own *w*. So to a Yolanda Yvonne Young, or a Yvette Yasmine Yates out there, can't you hear your letter clearly calling your name?

Why a Defender of the *R*?

My earlier diatribe against the French language accused the French of wasting freighter-loads of consonants. The formula I quoted from my French class days was that only the consonants found in the word CAREFUL were sounded at the end of a French word (and not always then). You notice that even the French have a fondness for the letter *r*. It is one of the four consonants which get some respect in their language. Pity that we who share the English mother tongue cannot learn this one lesson of respect from those folks across the Channel.

We have routinely scattered the letter *r* across the words in our vocabulary, but have permitted many among us to go merrily along ignoring them in what appears to be a careless fashion. Equally frustrating is that we stand idly by as those same people plop an *r* on the ends of all sorts of words where it clearly does not appear! What gives with the disappearing and intrusive letter *r*?

This linguistic intrigue is rooted in two words most of us have never heard: "rhotic" and "non-rhotic," from the Greek letter *rho*. These obscure linguistic terms divide our English language into two very large and common categories. We all speak one version or the other. Each of us has also developed an ear for pronunciations which miss an *r* on the end of a printed word, or which add an *r* where none occurs. Until this moment, most of you will not have been given the chance to identify these spoken English classes by name.

In rhotic variations of English, the letter *r* is almost always pronounced in a hard and distinct fashion (pronunciation symbol \r\). None of us would miss the r-sound in such words as *red, rarity*, or *grow*. This pronunciation scheme is the most common variant found in the U.S. and Canada. These English-speakers will also sound the *r* in *car* and both *r*'s in *margarine*. There are regions of the U.S., though, who do not sound these *r*'s. They are part of those who speak the non-rhotic variation of English.

From New England down through the New York City area and a small section of the South, one finds non-rhotic pronunciation patterns. The South was once generally non-rhotic, but in recent decades this type of speech has declined.

In this minority version of American speakers, the rule is that an internal letter *r* is not pronounced unless it is immediately followed by a vowel (initial *r*'s are pronounced). Non-rhotic variations are the most common in the UK, New Zealand, and Australia. A notable exception would be the Scots, who mostly speak rhotically.

This variation is not so much a dialect as it is an accent, or a limited pattern of pronunciation. Read aloud the following sentence and see how many of the *r*'s you sound:

"I got into my car, drove to the store, and bought some bottled water and watery soup."

If you are a rhotic speaker, you fully pronounced the letter *r* in every word in all positions. A non-rhotic speaker would probably not sound the *r* in *car, store,* or *water,* but would for *drove* and *watery.* A slight change would have them pronouncing the *r* in *car*: "*I got into my car and drove to the store.*" Here the word is followed by a vowel, in this case in the next word, so the *r* would be sounded.

The classic New England pronunciation test is: "*Park the car in Harvard Yard,*" spoken by the non-rhotic as "Pahk the cah in Hahvahd yahd." Or another classic from Down East: "Bah Hahbah" for Bar Harbour, Maine.

I can recall on my first few trips to New York City, when leaving Midtown to go to the airport, it paid to say, "I'm going to La-guad-ia (rather than LaGuardia)" to the cab driver, making it appear I was a local. Otherwise, the trip could include a scenic tour of Flatbush by way of the Brooklyn Tunnel. What we think of as "The New York City accent" is non-rhotic.

When the *r* is in the middle of the word but ends a syllable, it may not be pronounced by British speakers. *Parliament* would sound like "Pah-le-ment" by a British speaker, rather than the rhotic "Par-le-ment." Try your hand at how most British, New Englanders, and other East Coast speakers would handle the *r*'s in this sentence: "*Go to the row at the rear of the theatre to hear the gorilla.*" One of the most awkward of these pronunciations I have heard occurs often on one TV cooking show when the chef with a NYC accent cautions cooks to "be caa-ful" when handling a hot item. It is extremely difficult to pronounce *careful* without sounding the *r*!

The earliest basis for this benign neglect of the *r* is what one might call the "educated English" of the British Isles. Known as "Received Pronunciation," it is the spoken English that has long been perceived as prestigious among British accents. This accent has also been known as "The Queen's (or King's) English," "BBC English", and "Oxford English."

For the British, this non-rhotic pronunciation pattern models education and good taste.

By my rough calculation, just all New Yorkers combined will ignore the existence of about two-hundred million *r*'s in any 24-hour period. Add the New Englanders, the British and non-rhotics from throughout the Empire to this total and you are talking real avoidance. But, there is some small balance in this problem. Non-rhotic speakers often just plop an *r* here and there in words, even when there is none in the spelling. Linguists assign an erudite name for such a phenomena, but I just call the habit irritating.

First, the "Linking R." This occurs in most (but not all) non-rhotic dialects of English. When a word that ends with an *r*-sound precedes a word that begins with a vowel, the *r*-sound will actually be pronounced at the beginning of the second word, not at the end of the first. For example, the *r* in *here* would not be pronounced in *"Here they are,"* because it is followed by a consonant. But, it would be pronounced in *"Here I am,"* since the *r*-sound is followed by a vowel. Or, the *r* in *far* would not be pronounced unless it were followed by something like *"far away"* or *"far off."*[40]

It would certainly take a sensitive ear in these instances to tell whether the *r* is being sounded at the end of the first word or at the beginning of the following word. The experts on this topic suggest that the first word has a non-rhotic pronunciation as it would be in isolation, and that the hard sound comes at the beginning of the trailing vowel word. That's just embarrassing to the *r*, don't you see? The tough and proud letter positions himself just at the right point and the speaker ignores the *r*'s careful preparation and positioning. It's like a careless driver ignoring a traffic control officer positioned at a dangerous intersection. Only linguistic chaos can come from the growth of this dialect.

The same *Wikipedia* article explains the vagaries of the "Intrusive R." Some (but not all) dialects that possess the "Linking R" also possess "Intrusive R." In such a dialect, "An epenthetic (that is, a sound that is not actually there) is added after a word that ends in a non-high vowel or glide if the next word begins with a vowel, regardless of whether the first word historically ended with (an *r*-sound) or not." In plain language, some people just stick an *r* into places they were just never intended to be. Sure, the same people just ignore the poor *r* all over the place, gather up a few, and just plunk them rather willy-nilly at the ends of unsuspecting words.

The following list of examples will help you grasp the range of this blasé disregard for the *r*'s self-determination:

- "I saw(r) a film today."
- "Never use vodka(r) in case of snake bite."
- "The law(r) is the law!" (The insistency here should be obvious to even one who is not obsessive-compulsive.)
- "I think Donna(r) is here." (Would that be someone from the ill-fated Donner party?)
- "That's the idea(r) of leaving now."
- "There's an orchestra(r) in rehearsal." (That one is almost as tough to say as "caa-ful.")
- "Sure, mama(r), I love you."
- "That's the quickest way to Florida(r), isn't it?"

So, here's the good news for the battered *r*. When we deduct all these linking and intrusive *r*'s sown liberally amid non-deserving soil, we might have the daily damage to this robust letter down to a few hundred-million a day.

If we work from the premise that written language generally reflects the original spoken language sounds, what gives with all those neglected *r*'s and the addition of these ghost *r*'s? It's a perfectly lovely consonant. It serves a distinctive and unique sound in spoken English. Why have such a large number of English-speaking people choosing to embarrass and belittle such a hard-working letter?

Granted, the *r* is no *w*. The harsh sound it represents will never win a pleasant-to-the-ear award. The "r-r-r" sound is really pretty grating to the ear. That's certainly true in comparison to the beautiful, comforting "o-o-o" of the *w*. In truth, when one takes vocal lessons, the music instructor is diligent in making certain the singer does all he can to eliminate that hard-*r* sound from his diction. Words like *world* or *hear* are to be sung "wuh-ld" and "hee-uh." I guess the vocalist is taught to become more non-rhotic? Wait a minute! Could it be it was the vocal teachers around the world who started all this neglect of the letter *r*?

So, Ronald or Ryan, you see the challenge you have if you choose to defend your favorite letter? Someone must take up the challenge, and sooner than later. Millions of letters are finding their way to the alphabet trash bin each day. If you accept this difficult mission, may the fah-ss be with you!

You May Be from the South if....

Many Southern-born folk work hard to get rid of any evidence of their Southern dialect. They do this for a variety of reason, most of which tend to be economic. They wish to fit in better in Chicago or Los Angeles or New York City. Efforts include such things as taking classes to lose the accent, or simply watching the evening news and mimicking the newscaster. Those who deliver the national news are taught to embrace a kind of accent-neutral English, which tends to be a rather Midwestern dialect.

I have long enjoyed trying to place geographically the dialect of someone I've just met. I can often come close. But, I am sometimes surprised when someone tells me they are from Mississippi or Alabama, and they sound very Midwestern. I have had some people explain the classes they've taken or the hours of practice in front of the TV. Listen carefully, though, and you will often hear their fatal flaw: the Telltale-D!

People from below the Mason-Dixon Line put a *d* in the word *important*. They substitute it for the first *t*: "im-por-dant." I have found that this regional practice is one oddity that slips through their efforts to transform their accent. Whenever you hear that misplaced *d*, you may be fairly certain they grew up in the South.

I thought for years that the Telltale-D was also a similar test in the word *business*. Some Southerners say, "bid-ness." Turns out, though, this pronunciation is common also in urban jargon, by people not necessarily from the South.

Why a Defender of the *Y*?

Yolanda and Yvette, you have a similar challenge ahead if you accept the challenge to defend your favorite letter. It has endured significant neglect and inattention since its arrival in our alphabet as early as Roman times. I have been so moved by the plight of the *y* that I am going to suggest in Chapter Fwrteen that we put the poor, one-legged letter out of its misery. I will be recommending, as part of my overhaul of the English alphabet, the elimination of the *y*.

So, if you are going to set out to mount a defense of the *y*, you had best get organized and armed quickly. My legions will soon begin the first transformation of our alphabet in more than sixteen-hundred years and you may not have a letter to defend.

Chapter Thirteen

The Embarrassing Names of the Other Letters of the Alphabet (and Suggested Changes)

Who named the letters in the English alphabet? What committee gathered many centuries ago, maybe along the banks of the Thames, and debated and argued until they agreed that the *a* should be called "eh" rather than "ah?" My chapter on the history of the letter *w* did not look at how the letters of our alphabet were *named*, and by whom. As one looks at the scheme of names we use for our letters, we might wonder how efficient is our system? Our name for the *w* seems to be the only one that has any logic.

Unfortunately, my admiration for the name "Double-U" has not been shared by all. The nineteenth century satirist Ambrose Bierce found little to appreciate in this letter name. In his cynical *Devil's Dictionary* he observed:

"W (double U) has, of all the letters in our alphabet, the only cumbrous name, the names of the others being monosyllabic. This advantage of the Roman alphabet over the Grecian is the more valued after audibly spelling out some simple Greek word, like *epixoriambikos*. Still, it is now thought by the learned that other agencies than the difference of the two alphabets may have been concerned in the decline of 'the glory that was Greece' and the rise of 'the grandeur that was Rome.' There can be no doubt, however, that by simplifying the name of W (calling it 'wow,' for example) our civilization could be, if not promoted, at least better endured."

Poor Ambrose Gwinnett Bierce. With initials like A.G.B., I am afraid he must have had a bit of monogram envy. No wonder he had the nickname "Bitter Bierce." Just think how much less painful and brighter his life could have been for him if his parents had named him Ward, or Wheatly, or Will, or even Woody. See how those names tend to soften a person? I believe the only man's name which is more gentle than one beginning with a *w* is "Skippy." Skippy Bierce would have given us a totally different body of Literature-by-Bierce. Parents, be careful naming your children, and never be afraid of the *w*-names (except maybe Werner or Wilhelm...some nationalities just don't carry it off as well as others).

As I was about to write before Ambrose Bierce butted in, when the letter came into our language to represent the sound previously covered by a *uu* or a *vv*, the question must have been, "What shall we call this new letter?" Why not name it for its very function and call it a "Double-U?" That simple solution brought a whole new dimension to the naming of letters. All other letters coming into English by way of Latin had carried names assigned long before the creation of the *w*.

The English language was first written in the Anglo-Saxon futhorc runic alphabet, in use from the fifth century. That letter scheme was replaced by the Latin alphabet from about the seventh century on, although the two continued in parallel for some time.[41] So, the names given to the older letters in the Classic Latin alphabet were fixed and would be largely carried over as the names for our English letters as well. Those Classic Latin letter names were:

A = ā	I = ī	R = er
B = bē	K = kā	S = es
C = cē	L = el	T = tē
D = dē	M = em	V = ū
E = ē	N = en	X = ex
F = ef	O = ō	Y = ī Graeca
G = gē	P = pē	Z = zēta
H = hā	Q = qū	

Notice that the ancient Latin alphabet lacked a *j*, *u*, and *w*. The Latin *v* served for the sound ū.

Most of these letter names have been carried over for fourteen hundred years or so in the letter names in the English alphabet. So, must we assume that those profligate Romans, speaking and writing that dread Latin language, were given the privilege of setting our English letter names in concrete? Am I to understand that we brilliant, creative English-speaking people of the twenty-first century must blindly acquiesce to a system of letter names foisted upon us by a civilization that was upended by the Visigoths? Must Americans continue to parrot letter names bestowed upon us by a culture that pronounced "Vini, vidi, vici" as "weanie, weedie, weekie?" We have put men on the moon! Can't we come up with better names for the letters of our alphabet than the designations inherited from guys in togas? Don't you share my outrage? Bear with me cause I think we can do better than that.

So, what's the problem? The problem is our letter names, except for the clear and meaningful appellation called "Double-U," have little or no relationship to the actual function of that letter in our language. Take the *a*, for example. We call this letter an "ay." That name is actually two letters: *a* + *y* (or *e*). That sound never appears in the pronunciation of the *a* in any English word. The sound is generally either an ā (*brave*) or an ă (*hat*). Does it not make more sense for those of us who own our language to pronounce the name of that letter either an "eh" (rather than "ay") or an "aa?"

One more quick example. How about the letter *t*? We call it a "tee," which is, again, actually two letters: *t* + *e*. The *t* on its own never represents that sound in a word. It always signals the "tuh" sound, as in *time*. See where I am going here? The names for English letters to which we have been subscribing for fourteen centuries don't fit our language. Might have fit Latin, but not English.

Some decades ago the Roman Catholic Church found the courage to cut itself free from the Latin language in liturgy. Can't we muster the boldness to finally cut ourselves free from the demands of Classic Latin on our alphabet! Let's you and I give it a try.

First, you. Have you never wondered why we call an *e* an "ee" rather than, say, an "eh?" Or who decided we should call a *v* a "vee", rather than "vuh?" You know that Americans are pretty much alone at calling a *z* a "zee." Most of the rest of the English-speaking world refer to it as a "zed." Take a few moments and look objectively, deeply objectively for probably the first time in your life, at what we call the various letters in our alphabet. If you were challenged to call them something else….to rename our letters, what would you call them. I'll wait. This might take you a while. It requires you to not only think outside the box, but to pretend for a moment there is no box.

Thanks for doing that. That might have been one of the more liberating things you have ever done as an adult. Now, here are my recommendations for renaming our English alphabet. You will find that we have long been using double-letter combination sounds for essentially all our letters. In precious few instances do the letters represent that sound in print. I think you will find that my new names would more closely reflect the sound the letter represents in print.

Letter	Current Name	Recommended New Name
A	ay	aa (the long-a sound requires another vowel)
B	bee	buh
D	dee	duh
E	ee	eh (the long-e sound requires two *e*'s)
F	eff	fuh
G	gee	guh
H	aytch	huh
I	eye	ih
J	jay	juh
K	kay	kuh
L	ell	luh
M	em	muh
N	en	nuh
O	oh	oh (no change)
P	pee	puh
R	are	ruh
S	ess	suh
T	tee	tuh
U	you	uh (the long-u sound requires other letters)
V	vee	vuh
W	double-you	ooo
Z	zee (or zed)	zuh

First, please note that I am even recommending a change in the name of my favorite letter. I have no qualms about this. With the suggested change in the *u* name, a change in the Double-U is required. You will notice that the new *w* name is still the most beautiful and appealing of all the rest of our letter sounds. This name change moves the *w* from the most functional of the letter names to the most beautiful.

Go back over this list of suggested new names, speaking aloud the new letter names in order, as if you were a kindergartener reciting them aloud for the first time. The letter names are not as pleasant to the ear as the Latin names, are they? But, they reflect the sound the letter will most often make, on its own, in print. If we had learned this new naming scheme from our very first childhood alphabet lessons, it would not sound nearly as harsh.

Now, assuming there is no one within earshot, try singing aloud the "Alphabet Song" using the suggested name changes. If someone is close enough to overhear you, just tell them you recently lost your job at the post office and are having trouble remembering how to sing the alphabet song. As you begin, they will scurry away.

The song is still reasonably melodic isn't it? But, obviously by now you have noticed the missing letters. What about the missing letters? They have not been included among the renaming scheme because I am now preparing to recommend we prune the *c*, *q*, *x*, and *y* from our English alphabet as unnecessary in representing our spoken language. Yes, I believe we can eliminate these four letters and realize greater clarity and genuine letter economies. I am not, however, advocating sending any of the letter savings to the Poles since all the reduction is in consonants rather than vowels. The last thing the Polish language needs is large shipments of *c*'s, *q*'s, *x*'s, and *y*'s from America. That's how the French got them into trouble in the first place!

If you have had the courage to bear with me during this renaming exercise, you may be ready now to continue our efforts at reclaiming our English alphabet from the Romans. In order to do that, though, we must get serious about the order in which they handed down their alphabet. Why did they decide to begin with an *a* and end with a *z*? It most probably goes back to the order of the Greek alphabet.

Those of you who had to memorize the Greek alphabet as a pledge in a fraternity or sorority may recall you noticed there was some similarities between our alphabet and the Alpha-to-Omega letters in Greek. When Rome overran the Greek Empire, they pretty much adopted everything Greek as their very own, except baklava. They went a different way there and that apparently led to the unfortunate eventual development of pineapple pizza. The Romans did have the courage to rename the Greek letters, pretending they had no idea the Greek and Latin schemes were similar. My point is, if those people who worshiped emperors had the chutzpah to rename the letters they borrowed from the Greeks, can't we muster enough pluck to do the same?

In addition to the renaming, the People of the Boot were creative enough to produce their own new symbols for sounds in the Latin language. They didn't just assume the Greeks knew best with symbols like Δ, Θ, Σ, and Ω. Again, can't we embrace that same kind of freedom in deciding which letters we need, and maybe add a letter here or there that better serves us? If your answer is no, you are becoming a real drag here. If you are adventurous enough, let's move on to reorganizing our pruned, renamed alphabet and to seeing if we have need for anything beyond the current proposal of twenty-two letters.

Chapter Fwrteen

English Alphabet Letter Order (and Suggested Changes)

For those of you still with me (maybe we'll talk later about those cowards who bailed on us after the last chapter), we have to take a serious look at the order we have long used for the English alphabet. I have searched the scriptures of all the world's great religions and can find no divine decree anywhere that ties us to our A-to-Z order.

The alphabet has often been described as an arbitrary collection of symbols representing an arbitrary collection of sounds. Its order is equally random. We have already seen that such an arbitrary order has been passed down to us from Greek to Latin to Anglo-Saxon, eventually to Modern English. No substantive changes in how we organize our letters have been made in thousands of years. Does the current order of the English alphabet still serve us well, or are there changes one can make.

In order to steel your resolve as we approach this sacred moment, remember the typewriter (and computer) keyboard. The QWERTY keyboard arrangement on a typewriter was created in the 1860s by Christopher Sholes, a newspaper editor who lived in Milwaukee. There are several reasons advanced for why this order was adopted. For our needs right now, though, it is just important to note that Sholes and early typists were not tied to our common alphabetical order. They found a better way. Let's you and I have a go at this also.

First, you. Look over the English alphabet and see if you can make any sense of the order we have been handed. Do you see any rhyme or reason for the vowels and the consonants being intermingled? It appears that some of our less used letters have been placed at the end of the list where they belong. Do you know what is our most frequently used consonant? It's the *t*, and it is relegated to a spot near the end. Can you devise a letter order that honors such things as letter function (vowel or consonant) and frequency of use, placing the hardworking letters first and the filler letters last? What would your new order look like? Give it a shot. Meanwhile, I'll go back over my list to see if mine needs any last minute changes. Mine needs at least one letter addition, and I must find a proper symbol to use for my new "chuh."

Are you done? Does your letter order list include all twenty-six letters, or did you drop the *c*, *q*, *x*, and *y* as I suggested? When we drop those superfluous sound-symbols, it gives new value to a few other letters. As you did this exercise, didn't you get a sense that you are plowing new linguistic ground? Don't you feel a bit of a pioneer, not just settling for the territory you have been handed, but moving boldly ahead into new terrain?

Our lists must take into account the frequency of use of each letter. You may be able to find a variety of letter frequency lists online. Is there one impeccable source for this information? Has any organization made a living assigning frequency of use to our alphabet? Yep, *Scrabble*. The inventors of that international board game apparently did some significant research in preparation for assigning a value to the letter tiles. What would their general letter order be, based on the number of times each letter appears in our language? Here the irony is that the higher the letter value in *Scrabble*, the lower that letter would be in our new alphabet word order.

The values placed on the *Scrabble* tiles are (with the number of tiles for the letter):

- One point – E (12), A (9), I (9), O (8), N (6), R (6), T (6), L (4), S (4), U (4)
- Two points – D (4), G (3)
- Three points – B (2), C (2), M (2), P (2)
- Four points – F (2), H (2), V (2), W (2), Y (2)
- Five points – K (1)
- Eight points – J (1), X (1)
- Ten points – Q (1), Z (1)

Using this list by itself, a rearranged letter order, in descending frequency of use, would look something like: E, A, I, O, N, R, T, L, S, U, D, G, B, C, M, P, F, H, V, W, Y, K, J, X, Q, Z. Any letter here that its order/frequency surprises you? This would group the vowels (except for the U) at the first, leading through the consonants to two of the letters I am recommending we drop. Try reading this letter order aloud. Really sounds strange, doesn't it. Shows the amount of alphabetic nonsense we have been hauling around in our brain since childhood. One test law enforcement officers ask of suspected drunk drivers is repeating the letters of the alphabet. Go ahead and commit this order to memory. If you are stopped, rattle it off. Then, one, insist you are not drunk; two, tell him you prefer this order to the antiquated one he insists upon. This is civil disobedience at its best! Please do not use my name, however, at your arraignment.

I have chosen one useful list of letter frequencies from those available online. Here are the percentage values that list assigns.[42] See how this compares to the *Scrabble* people's research.

A – 8.17%	N- 6.75%
B- 1.49 %	O- 7.51%
C- 2.78%	P- 1.93%
D- 4.25%	Q- 0.10%
E-12.70%	R- 5.99%
F- 2.23%	S- 6.33%
G- 2.02%	T- 9.06% (nearly one of every
H- 6.09%	10 letters in English is a T!)
I- 6.97%	U- 2.76%
J- 0.15% (only Q, X, and Z are	V- 0.98%
lower)	W- 2.36%
K- 0.77%	X- 0.15%
L- 4.03%	Y- 1.97%
M- 2.41%	Z- 0.07%

Any eye-openers there for you? Certainly the frequency of the *t* and the infrequency of the *j* lead my list of surprises. I would love to add the *j* to my list of deletions from the alphabet, but the *g* just will not fill all the needs of both the *g* and the *j*. The *g* can be both hard, as in *garter* or soft, as in *gym*. The *j* will have to stay, even though it really doesn't carry much of the weight.

My *w* carries her weight rather nicely. She tucks in just behind the slowest vowel *(u)* and blows away the other consonant/vowel, the *y*. She also leaves many of the other consonant-only letters in her dust. Pretty frisky filly, eh?

Before I give you my complete, renamed, reordered, pruned English alphabet, let's deal with those letters I think we no longer need. First the *c*. This may be the easiest of the selections to delete.

We all know the *c* represents two sounds: the k-sound in words like *cat* and *cork*. That latter word gives it all away. We don't need the *c* for the k-sound. We already have the *k* for the k-sound. Duh. This is the more common of the two sounds the *c* represents. It, of course, also is used sometimes to represent the s-sound in words like *cent, citizen* and *circle*. Pretty simple parallel here to the k-sound. We don't need the *c* for the s-sound. The *s* herself does a right fine job representing herself. Though the *c* may be the eleventh most frequently used letter in the English language, unfortunately it is only a pretender to that honor. It is with sincere apologies to my wife Carol that we can get along quite nicely without the *c*. See if you have any trouble reading these words:

kabinet	sentury	klose
kalendar	sinema	synik
krust	klamor	sykle
sertifikate	komedy	barnikal

Have you found the one problem the elimination of the *c* will cause us? Check your dictionary and you will find one *c*-combination for which we have no other letter. It's the *ch* sound, as in *church*. No *k* or *s* sound will help here, unless we wish to adopt the Scottish word for *church*: *kirk*. No, we have a dilemma which I would now like to solve. English needs a new letter. This would be the first new letter to be added to our alphabet in thousands of years. Let's live dangerously and birth a new English letter in our alphabet. Kind reader, let me introduce you to the "chuh:" Ç (small "chuh" is ç).

We can borrow this letter from the Cyrillic alphabet. The ç (ç) is a letter which appears in Albanian, Turkish, Azerbajani, Turkmen, Tatar, and Kurdish languages, and occasionally in a number of other languages. It can represent a variety of sounds, depending upon the tongue. I select this particular character to represent the ch-sound in English, not because of any comparable role it might play in another language, but because it is a really cute letter. I think that little tail, (which is known as a *cedilla*) on our letter C (c) looks just perfect for our sound "chuh." What's more, it appears to me from the past few presidential campaigns that many Americans are clamoring for us to become a bit more like the people on the Continent. There you go, the languages of the Continent seem to be very fond of the letter ç.

So, the C (c) goes, and welcome ç (ç), the "Chuh." This character is easily accessible among the "symbols" you can choose to insert from most word processing software. It is found among the Cyrillic letters. We'll have to use that method until the rest of the publishing world catches up with you and me and includes the ç in future font selections. See if you don't think this letter works quite nicely in these English words (with some of my other substitute letters included):

çurç	çestnut	çukle
çanse	çiken	çosen
çarter	çit- çat	çuk roast
çess	çokolate	çildish

Did you have any trouble with those? I didn't think you would. You are a reader who has toughed it out to this point in the book and are reaping the rewards of your intellectual diligence. Take a moment and reward yourself with whatever you eat or drink to bring you comfort. I'll wait. You *will* need fortification. We must next deal with the surgical removal of three more letters from our alphabet. This could get messy.

Let's now get rid of the *q*. Again, this is not a particularly difficult task. The sound represented by the *k* ("kuh"), especially when used other than at the beginning of a word, is the same sound represented by the *q*: *torque, lacquer, mannequin, equine.* These are just as easily understood as *tork, lakker* (need the two *k*'s here to change the a-sound), *mannekin*, and *ekwine*.

That final word, points up the other sound the *q* can represent, as in: *quick, quinine, quiet, question.* Instead of the "kuh," this sound requires the k-w combination, the "kuh + ooo." This slight additional use of our favorite letter, in these rare instances (the *q* is the second least used letter in our alphabet after the *z*) is only a minor adjustment in our letter economy: *kwik, kwinine, kwiet,* and *kwestion.*

Two down, two to go (plus we've added one letter). How about the *x*? Why should we eliminate this third-least-used letter in English (along with the *j*)? Doesn't it represent a unique sound in our language? Is there anything that can easily replace this letter? I think so.

Grab your dictionary and look through the couple of pages of English words which begin with an *x*. Kwite an education, isn't it. From *Xanadu* to *Xylose*, essentially every word can just as easily be spelled with a *z*. The rare exceptions are those words which use the letter *x* itself in the word: *X-ray, X-rated.* So *xenophobe, xylophone*, and *xerography* can just as easily be spelled *zenophobe, zilophone* (next letter to go will be the *y*), and *zerography*. The other set of words would need to be spelled *eks-ray,* and *Eks-rated*. I could live with that slight change. I'd love to see the porno industry have to convert to *eks-Rated movies*, or *Triple EKS-movie*. It wouldn't hurt me in the least to see those blood-suckers have to suffer a bit for their kraft, even for their very eksistense.

But, wait a minute. Isn't that word *xerography* derived from the brand name *Xerox*? Yep. Under these proposed changes in the alphabet, those guys would either have to get used to our spelling their company name *Zeroks*, or they would have to sue us. I know that new spelling would make the Xerox people sound like some folks from another planet, but we all have to make sacrifices for the good of this alphabet revolution.

There, I've said it. We all must begin preparing for a bit of opposition to our suggested changes in the alphabet. There may be some people in America who do not see the need for these changes. I believe it is you text-messaging people who will need to lead the way for us in demonstrating the daily joys of the new alphabet. Just think of the reduction in stress in the children of future generations when they begin learning this new, user-friendly alphabet. You see, I am only doing all this for the children.

And finally, our children are simply not going to need the *y*. Why is that? As you may recall from my chapters on the history of our letters, this late arrival to the English alphabet has had a rather spotty history. Like the *w* it has labored as both a consonant and a vowel. The standard name for this letter is pronounced "wye." Why? It does not, of course, represent that sound in any word. First, it represents a double-e sound, especially when it is used as the first letter: *yard, year, yoke, young, yuck*. Are these words not easily understood as *eeard, eeear, eeoke, eeoung, eeuk*? It can represent that same sound later in a word also, as in *turkey* and *syrup*. Could we not live with *turkee* and *seerup*?

When appearing later in a word, the *y* often represents the ie-sound: *try, type, hype, cycle*, and *dye*. I submit to you that we could get along with *trie, tiepe, hiepe, siekle,* and *die.* But, oh, you protest, *die* already means something else! We can't have that! Oh, really. That shouldn't be any problem for those of us who have been living with *bass* (fish) and *bass* (low voice); *bow* (ribbon) and *bow* (bend at the waist); *desert* (arid place) and *desert* (to leave behind); *excuse* (forgive) and *excuse* (let leave); *house* (place you live) and *house* (to give someone a place to live); *rebel* (a breakaway figure) and *rebel* (the act of breaking away); *sewer* (one who sews) and *sewer* (soil pipe), and *wind* (a breeze) and *wind* (energize the clock). There are so many more problems in our language than any one person can ever address. If our children are to live in harmony with our language, they are going to have to put up with lots of loose (or is it *lose*?) ends.

Finally the *y* can also represent the short-*i* sound in words such as *system, typical,* and *polyp.* This one is fairly easy. Our kids will probably have less problem with *sistem, tipikal,* and *polip.*

So, there we are! We have eliminated four letters from the English alphabet as redundant and added one to pick up the leftover "chuh" sound with the deletion of the *c.* Thank you for your firm constitution in witnessing this delicate surgery on our alphabet. The actual surgery itself will be replayed sometime in the future on C-Span. Check your local listings for time and channel.

Where does that leave us, then? I am ready to unveil our newly created and diligently crafted English alphabet. It will reflect the new names we have assigned to each remaining letter. It will recognize the elimination of the four letters. We will inaugurate our newest English letter. And the *English Alphabet for the 21st Century* will be rearranged to reflect the frequency of use in print of each letter. Tuh-duh!

The English Alphabet for the 21ˢᵗ Century
("The E-Z Alphabet")

Letter	Letter Name	Frequency %	Letter	Letter Name	Frequency %
E	eh	12.70%	M	muh	2.41%
T	tuh	9.06%	W	ooo	2.36%
A	aa	8.17%	F	fuh	2.23%
O	oh	7.51%	G	guh	2.02%
I	ih	6.97%	P	puh	1.93%
N	nuh	6.75%	B	buh	1.49%
S	suh	6.33%	Ç	chuh	(unknown)
H	huh	6.09%	V	vuh	0.98%
R	ruh	5.99%	K	kuh	0.77%
D	duh	4.25%	J	juh	0.15%
L	luh	4.03%	Z	zuh	0.07%
U	uh	2.76%			

The Ç is placed in this sequence based on my best guess as to how often the ch-sound appears in English. The "E-Z Alphabet" name is derived from the first and last letters in the new alphabet.

Check your favorite letter in this list. Most of us have a favorite letter. It's the letter we would hang on our wall or have monogrammed on our sweater. How does your favorite letter fare under this new scheme? Are you surprised by how often, or how little your favorite letter appears in our language?

When you review this new order, does it seem like I might have concocted this new system just to prosper the *w*? My favorite letter certainly has prospered under this new alignment. It has moved up seven spots in the order and has a wonderful new name. Just think, the universal use of this system would have people throughout the English-speaking world saying "ooo" nearly every day. Every repeat of the "E-Z Alphabet" would include an "ooo." Don't you think this would make our nation a kinder, gentler place? "Ooo," sure it would. Give it a try yourself. Read through the new letter names in order and see if, once again, the *ɯ* isn't still the darling of the alphabet.

If you want to practice using the "E-Z Alphabet," try reading this twenty-first century version of a portion of the opening of our *Declaration of Independence*.

When in the kourse of human events it bekomes nesessari for one people to dissolve the politikal bands whiç have konnekted them with another and to assume

among the powers of the earth, the separate and ekwal station to whiç the Laws of

Nature and of nature's God entitle them, a desent respekt to the opinions of mankind rekwires that thei should deklare the kauses whiç impel them to the separation.

We hold these truths to be self-evident, that all men are kreated ekwal, that they are endowed by their Kreator with sertain unalienable Rights, that among these are Life, Liberti and the pursuit of Happiness. That to sekure these rights, Governments are instituted among Men, deriving their just powers from the konsent of the governed.

That whenever ani Form of government bekomes destruktive of these ends, it is the Right of the People to alter or to abolish it, and to institute new Government, laiing its foundation on suç prinsiples and organizing its powers in suç form, as to them shall seem most likeli to effect their Safety and Happiness.

Not too difficult, is it? In fakt, it is kwite easi. Eou are proving eourself eekwal to the task, and are now eligible for an "E-Z Alphabet Reader" sertifikate. Just design suç a sertifikate eourself on your komputer and print it out to displai on your wall.

I am hanging my sertifikate along side my large monogram *w*.

Mai the *w* be oooith eou!

ADDENDA

Answers to the "Letter Economy Exercise" (in Chapter Nine)

* * * *

English Words Which Should Be Spelled with a *ɯ*

Recommended Spelling / Current, Awkward Spelling / (No. of Vowels Saved)

adw	/ adieu / (2)	kwik	/ quick / (1)	pwl	/ pool / (1)
bwth	/ booth / (1)	kwk	/ kook / (1)	rwl	/ rule / (1)
cw	/ coo / (1)	lwz	/ lose / (1)	rwm	/ room / (1)
cwp	/ coop/coup / (1)	lws	/ loose / (2)	rwt	/ root / (1)
cwth	/ couth / (1)	lwp	/ loop / (1)	rwlet	/ roulette / (2)
ew	/ you / (1)	lwvr	/ louver / (2)	skwl	/ school / (1)
fwd	/ food / (1)	mwr	/ moor / (1)	spwn	/ spoon / (1)
flw	/ flew/flue / (1)	mws	/ moose / (2)	swn	/ soon / (1)
grwv	/ groove / (2)	mwt	/ moot / (1)	swt	/ soot / (1)
gwrmet	/ gourmet / (1)	mwv	/ move / (1)	swvenir	/ souvenir / (1)
gws	/ goose / (2)	nw	/ new / (1)	tw	/ two* / (1)
hwray	/ hooray / (1)	nwn	/ noon / (1)	twl	/ tool / (1)
jwse	/ juice / (1)	nwrish	/ nourish / (1)	twt	/ toot / (1)
jwl	/ jewel / (2)	pwr	/ poor / (1)	twth	/ tooth / (1)
kwak	/ quack / (1)	pwf	/ poof / (1)	twcan	/ toucan / (1)

W. Whoolery White

wz	/ whose / (1)	ywth	/ youth / (1)	<u>Tot. Vowels saved:</u> (61)
wlong	/ oolong / (1)	zw	/ zoo / (1)	* We'll still need a
wol	/ wool / (1)	zwt swt/ zoot suit / (2)		"too" spelling
wwzy	/ woozy / (1)			

Double-U Trivia

The Radio ɯ Band

The U.S. government began licensing radio stations in 1912, and what letters of the alphabet did our feds choose for the assigning of call letters to radio stations? The ɯ and the *k*. That's right, listeners all across regions of America would awaken each morning to the dulcet sounds of, "Good morning from WLGR, the voice of reason in the scenic Crustacean River Valley." Originally the letter assignments gave the ɯ to the people in the *east* (go figure the Feds), and the *k* to those remote, never-heard-from, western states. Why the ɯ in the states where people lived? How much more pleasant "WABC" sounds, than the harsh "KABC." Our favorite letter is always welcome to the ears, when pronounced correctly. *K*, not so much.

When the TV sitcom *WKRP in Cincinnati* was created, it could have been "KBOJ in Kansas City," but who would watch a show with such a harsh sound? If you want to launch a radio station with pizzazz, go for the ɯ, on the radio band from 75 to 111 GHz. The ɯ will be your friend, but the *k* will just make you look second class. After all, in the E-Z English Alphabet, the *k* edges out only the *j* and the *z* for last place. It's clear to me, our government has always been partial to the ɯ. How can it not be? She's a graphic designer's dream: balance, symmetry, even impulsive as she imposes herself into the space of narrower, less attractive letters.

ɯ on TV

If you were planning to start a new cable channel and could use only one letter, which would you choose? If you wanted a name that said free, fun-loving, bright and breezy, you would probably choose the *w*. That proved to be true in both Canada and Australia.

The W Network in Canada is a light, clean, fun entertainment channel. Nothing stodgy, nothing *X* (raunchy) *or Z* (science-fictiony like). If you want TV fare that says wholesome, you want the letter that initiates that word. Try the other English letters in your mind as stand-alone names for a cable network. Not so much there, is there? I could go with "The Ç Channel," but so few people know how to pronounce that yet. It does have a certain flair, though, doesn't it?

Then there's the W. Channel in Australia. I like the addition of the period. Gives the name a touch of finality, like "*The* Television Channel." Again, the creators of that network apparently envisioned a bright, breezy, pleasurable viewing experience. According to their website they, "Offer the very best in quality entertainment, because like you, we love to watch great television. *W.* We entertain." How could you name something like that the T. Network, or R. Network, or even the F. Network? Why don't any of those work? The *w* seems to be unique in her ability to comfort and charm. It's not just her looks, it's also her voice. One just loves to hear her say, "Ooo" at the start of any word.

The most charming sound in American television is *The We Channel for Women*, also known as *WeTV*. Creators could have chosen *SheTV*, or *HerTV*, but somehow those just don't work either. It's not just that *we* is more personal, it's also more pleasant to say and to hear. Call me crazy, but I think television loves the *w*. Vanna, is there a *w*? You bet there is!

<u>w</u> *in Other Entertainments*

The tagline for the Richard Quine 1974 movie *W* was, "*W*... suspense beyond words." How many movies can you recall which took the risk of resting on a one-word title? Of course there is the 2008 film *W* by Oliver Stone. That was easy since it was a trashing of the administration of "Dubya," President George Bush. I never saw that freak show, and not because I care much about what he had to say about Bush. I would not contribute the cost of admission to any movie that defames the letter *w*.

According to a list of one-letter film titles on *www.listology. com*, through 2004 there were only four letters for which a movie has not been named: *c*, *n*, *r*, and *t*. Which letter has enjoyed the most one-letter movie titles? *X*, of course, with seven not-so-memorable films. You will be pleased to hear that the prurient interests of those movies have been offset somewhat by the letter with the second most films: the *w*. In addition to the two mentioned above there were films by the Finnish director Taru Mäkelä in 1983 and a short by Lu Feit in 2003. Taste will out.

Our letter has appeal in many lands. There was a short-lived pop vocal duo in Japan called *W* (also known as "Double U" and "Double You."). The sound our letter *w* represents must also be pleasant to the ear of the Japanese? Turns out it is a fairly common sound in their spoken language. The vocal duo did well, though, not to choose the name *L*, don't you think? One of the most peculiar sounds in human language is a Japanese choir singing the "Harreruah Chorus."

Our favorite letter's impact is also felt in magazine publishing. When Oprah Winfrey was brassy enough to publish a magazine bearing only her initial, *O, the Oprah Magazine* she caused quite a stir. How presumptuous of her. The women's magazine even spun off *O, at Home*, a companion publication. Actually it was rather daring. I find that there are only four other English language magazines bold enough to try it with only a one-letter title. *D* magazine is a Dallas/Fort Worth area what's-happening monthly; *E: the Environmental Magazine* can't take the chance of letting the letter *e* stand on its own; and *M* magazine is a teen, celebrity fan occasional publication. I can't determine what the *M* in the title represents. I think it might just mean "magazine," to help the teeny boppers distinguish it from CDs and DVDs. That cell phone radiation scare on teenager's brains may deserve more attention than we have been paying it?

There is one more single-letter magazine title. It is *w*. Have you ever noticed this women's fashion monthly on the newsstands? It really stands out. It not only has flashy, glossy covers, but it is a large format periodical. You can't miss it amongst the other more humble publications. Its larger format permits it to insinuate itself into the shoppers vision, pushing aside the smaller, more delicate offerings. What a perfect magazine to be named *w*. It carries the proud tradition of our letter onto the shelves and racks of our nation. It pretty much just kicks butt when stacked up against *O*. Oprah, you should have used your second initial, rather than your first. The *w* might have made you some real money.

The National Association of "W" Lovers

Where would one go to join the National Association of "W" Lovers? Such an organization might be a desired outcome of my book. I can imagine that such a national group would grow from among you readers, especially any of you also blessed with the initials W.W.W. I can envision an annual convention of us *w*-3s, held yearly at Walla Walla, Washington (where else?).

But, alas, I am too late. *The Muppets* formed the group several years ago. The first meeting of the "Nation Association of 'W' Lovers" was held on *Sesame Street*, with the Muppet character Bert as the chairperson.[43]

The *Sesame Street* segment began with Bert's friend Ernie and five other characters talking with each other. Standing behind the podium, Bert gathers the group and the following meeting of the Association got underway:

* * * * *

(***Ernie***, a boy, and five other men talk to one another.)

Bert: All *right, all right, all right, everybody. Settle down. Come on now.*
(clears his throat)
Welcome to the weekly meeting of the National Association of "W" Lovers.
We are gathered here today to pay tribute to that great letter "W" and the wondrous sound it makes... "Wuh!"
Isn't that lovely? "Wuh!" Yeah, it makes the heart pound faster. All right.
Now if you all turn to page four in the manual, we will sing the club's song.
All right, everybody, turn to page four. That's it. All right. Now is everybody ready? Here we go.

(Music starts)

I'll begin. You can join in later. Here we go.
(*sung*)
Oh, what is the letter we love?
What sound are we extra fond of?

W. Whoolery White

It's not any trouble
You know it's a "W"
When you hear "Wuh-wuh-wuh-wuh!"
Without this fine letter
You couldn't say "wash"
Or "witch," "wax," or "wiggle"
My gosh! Huh!
There wouldn't be "wet," "warm," or "walrus"
Oh wow!
There wouldn't be "wood"
Would there now? Uh-uh!
Without this great "Wuh" sound
Well, "wink" would be "ink"
And "week" would be "eek"
Don't you see? Of course.
A fine word like "waffle"
Would turn out just "awful"
Oh, "W's" grand as can be
(All right, everybody!)

(Ernie, the boy, and the five other men sing along with Bert.)

All: *So what is the letter we love?*
The sound that we're extra fond of?
It's not any trouble
You know it's a "W"
When you hear "Wuh-wuh-wuh-wuh!"
Bert: *(One more time!)*
All: *When you hear "Wuh-wuh-wuh-wuh!"*
(Music ends)
Bert: *Oh wow! That was wonderful!*[44]

Bert got it pretty much right on the money. What other of our letters could send such ecstasy through the heart of a puppet? How could a creature with a cloth heart develop such a love and respect for the *w*? There is just something deep within all creatures, whether of skin, fur, or cloth, that thrills at the sound of this letter. Even a dog says "woof!"

But, the song would have been even more rousing if the real sound of the *w* had been used: "ooo." How much more captivating the line would have been as, "When you hear 'woo-woo-woo-woo'!" But, I'm not complaining. When you have the Muppets and Sesame Street out front in the campaign to crown the *w* as our most beloved letter, this charter member of the club is not going to quibble.

w the Chemical Element

How many of you recall having to suffer through the memorization of the chemical elements table in high school? Let's see how your memory has held up. There is a metal element with the symbol *w*. Do you recall which one it is? I'll wait while you look it up.....that's right, it's tungsten. How did tungsten get such a letter designation, and why is this such a big deal for my favorite letter?

Tungsten comes from the Swedish word meaning "hard" or "heavy stone." In languages other than ours, the mineral is known as Wolfram. It is from that word that tungsten gets its element letter.

The metal tungsten is perfectly represented by the dynamic *w*. Of all the metals in pure form, tungsten has the highest melting point (6,192°F), lowest vapor pressure, and highest tensile strength. It also has the lowest coefficient of thermal expansion of any pure metal. Therefore, alloying small quantities of tungsten with steel greatly increases its toughness. Two of the common uses of this near indestructible metal are in light bulb and cathode-ray tube elements.

One might say *w* lights the world, both as an element and as a letter. In fact, scientists apparently were so distraught that this letter had been taken, they imitated the *w* by using two *u*'s for symbols for a couple newly discovered elements: *uun* for ununnilium (1987) and *uub* for ununbium (1996). When it comes to the Double-U, some are even satisfied with near greatness.

* * * * *

The Real Cause of
"Vorld Var Tvoo"

Do you ever get tired of hearing the endless theories of why the Roman Empire fell? Some say it was the moral decline. Others suggest it was because the empire got too unwieldy to govern. Yet others proclaim it was personal greed and financial collapse. Let's just agree that it was undoubtedly a broad, complex matrix of socio-political issues which resulted in Italy today grasping the handles of the tattered portmanteau of a once-great empire. Either that or it might have been global warming.

I also find a bit wearisome the seemingly inexhaustible catalogue of reasons for the outbreak of World War II. Who's right? Those who claim it was the inevitable result of the worldwide financial collapse during the Great Depression? Or do you agree with those who point to the rise of totalitarian, militaristic regimes in Germany, Italy and Japan? Or, possibly, you are onboard with those who theorize that it was the result of rapid growth in numbers of people who accepted the political remedies offered up by the claims of Nazism and Fascism. There is a growing clamor from those who would blame it also on global warming.

Well, I have no revelations about the demise of Rome, but my research has turned up a disturbing conversation involving Adolph Hitler and one of his closest friends. I believe that discussion in 1923 may well have been a seminal moment in the mind of the man who engineered the Third Reich. See if you don't agree that I have found the real cause of World War II.[45]

The Real Cause of Vorld Var Tvoo

He didn't plan to be a ruthless despot. If he were to be world renown, given half a chance, he would have preferred to have been known as an accomplished artist….a painter. Adolph Hitler as a young man in Vienna was gaining some reputation for his artistic talent. Though he had begun selling some of his paintings and post cards, the high school dropout was eventually denied admission to the Vienna Academy of Fine Arts (in 1907 and 1908, at the ages of eighteen and nineteen years). His rejections were accompanied by letters citing his "unfitness for painting."

As he walked away from the marble entrance of that venerated institution after his second rejection, he took out his brush and oils, and with one moment of grand defiance, scrawled across a portion of its austere façade, *"Max Ernst Farben durch Zahlen!"* ("Max Ernst paints by numbers!") Satisfied that he had evened the score with the Academy, the self-styled "Misunderstood Artist" enlisted in the Bavarian army in 1914.

His career in The Great War was rather unspectacular. He fell into disfavor early on with his commanding officer when Adolph speculated that all this trouble between European nations, "Can probably be laid at the feet of global warming." Captain Hauptmann Ungeschickt didn't know what the hell (*hölle*) Hitler was talking about, so he had him quickly shipped off to the French border. It was there he saw action in the infamous Battle of Quiche Lorraine.

The military tactic introduced in that *mêlée* (melee) saw German troops by night scatter small egg and schnitzel pies across wide expanses of No Man's Land. They hoped to lure French troops from their foxholes, to sure obliteration. This ploy failed miserably, however. The early morning dew proved to be too much for the lard-poor crusts, leaving soaked entrees that even a hungry Frenchman would not eat. The French cannot be fooled with mediocre pastry. The obsessive-compulsive Germans met bitter defeat as they left their places of protection to police the messy grounds with rakes and garbage cans.

As a result of his involvement in that military disaster, Hitler never gained the rank of even a full corporal. His two combat wounds involved being shot in the leg, and temporary blinding by Mustard Gas. He was determined to create a more commanding presence for himself before he was discharged back into society. The low-ranking corporal had lain awake long nights trying on nicknames which might toughen his image in the eyes of more accomplished men of the world. Rejecting such considerations as "Short Stuff," "Nugene the Turk," "Plentius Maximus," and "Skippy the Lion Hearted," he settled on the sobriquet "Herr Wolf." *Adolph* in Old High German meant "Noble Wolf." His fearsome persona had just been born.

Once discharged he chose the exciting city of Munich for his new home. Associations came quickly, but Adolph grew steadily disappointed and distant as one new acquaintance after another refused to call him "Herr Wolf." He spent his days alone in the beautiful Westpark, drawing around the outline of his hand, and coloring in the fingernails with either Burnt Sienna or Raw Umber. Overhearing his landlord one evening refer to him as "That guy in Rm. 212 with the limp and the squint," he nearly surrendered to a life of obscurity and defeat. Then he met the man who was to change his and Germany's future.

Kristof Führerbunker was a successful printer in Munich. Walking from his home on Hansa Strasse to his business across the park, he one day happened upon Adolph doodling

on his sketch pad. (There were no public *toilettenartikels*....
toilets... in the park in those days.) In need of someone in the art
department at his greeting card company, Führerbunker offered
the job to Hitler. That was the big break Herr Wolf had been
waiting for. He was now an artist at *Unglück* ("Tough Luck")
Greeting Card Co.

In just a few months Hitler was promoted to head of the
sympathy card division. In 1921 he designed an award-winning
sympathy card. It featured a grieving widow, kneeling beside the
graveside of her recently departed husband. The caption read,
"Besser als hier, Stuttgart!" ("Better here than Stuttgart!"). In
addition to a 9000-mark first prize ($1 American), the witty
caption earned Adolph a nomination for consideration as "The
Top German Humorist of the twentieth century." He was
awarded the prize nearly ten years later after no other names
had been placed in nomination.

By 1921 Hitler's new image as artist/humorist permitted
him opportunities to speak to large gatherings around the city.
He proved to be a popular and proficient speaker. Newspaper
accounts record some of his topics: "Bismarck: The Prussian
and the Pastry," *"Here's* Your Treaty of Versailles," "Don't
Speak of Poison Gas As If It's a Bad Thing," and "Low-Risk
Development Opportunities in Czechoslovakia." Herr Wolf's
career was finally getting on track. Who could have guessed
the impact of one innocent conversation he was to have in 1923.

Hitler's newest friend was Dietrich Eckart, one of the
founders of the German Workers' Party. Dietrich had just
returned from an extended trip to London. He had gone there
with the intentions of researching how the British had increased
per-capita beer consumption by nearly 30% by the launching of
weekly dart tournaments in their public houses. While watching
a particularly noisy match one Friday evening at the *Golden*

Hind in Portsmouth, he was invited into a free round of Guinness stout. Immediately changing his plans for a quick return to Germany, he spent several more months learning the ways of the Brits and getting much more familiar with Irish stout.

Upon Echart's return to Munich, he visited Hitler one evening to share what he had learned in England. Adolph lived above a *snell imbiss* (fast food place) specializing in currywurst. The fumes of the spicy curry sauce wafted up through the open gridiron floor grate, leaving the entire apartment (and Adolph) with the distinct odor of an Indian street vendor.

"Velcome home, Dietrich, my dear friend!," Hitler greeted. "You must tell me of your journeys among our cowardly adversaries in England."

"*Guten abend*, Adolph! It has been so many months since we last talked. I have much to share."

"Please, Dietrich, call me Herr Volf! "Adolph' died on the Vestern Front, in the Battle of Somme!"

"As you wish, Herr Wolf. I bring you some important....." Echart began, but Hitler interrupted.

"Vait a minute! Did you just call me "Herr Wolf," rather than "Herr Volf? Vhy do you insult me by mispronouncing my nickname?"

"But Adolph....or Herr Wolf....that is what I have come to tell you," he offered in defense. "I have come from secret meetings in the land of our enemies in the West. I have uncovered a wicked and dastardly plot against all in Germany and Austria!"

"There, you did it again! I am Herr Volf, not "Herr Wolf," Hitler nearly screamed through the fresh whiff of curry up through the grate. "Don't you mean 'a vicked and dastardly plot? Vhy vould you mock me in such a shameless vay? And vhy do you sound so funny?"

"But, Adolph, please listen! I have heard with my own ears of an ancient deceit, lead by a small group of shop owners in Britain, to humiliate all who speak our language. Vee have been hoodvinked by all in the Vest, I mean West, who originally sent us that Trojan Horse of a letter *vay* (W)!"

"Dietrich, you are beside yourself. Vhat has der *vay* got to do vith anything?," Hitler pleaded.

"But, mien Volf, the letter was never a *vay*! They sent us one of their alphabet letters they knew was a "double –uyuh," what they call a "double-u," and told us it was to be pronounced 'vay'!"

"Shut your *pie mund* (pie hole), mein freund! That cannot be. Vee have been pronouncing the *W* as "vay" since before Hildegard of Bingen had wisions….er…I mean visions. How could vee have been duped by people so plain and dowdy that they pack kidneys into pastry? Vee should have viped them all out in the Great Var!"

Echart was becoming frustrated by Hitler's hysterical interruptions. He moved his chair farther from the grate, thereby clearing his eyes of the sting from the curry odor below. Insisting on quiet, he explained the following.

Dietrich was participating in a heated game of darts at the Bagel and Lox pub near Kings Cross Station when his feathered shaft ricocheted off another dart and landed near a door to a private area in the rear of the pub. As he leaned down to retrieve the instrument, he clearly heard a voice through the door saying, "…And can you believe those stupid Germans have still not caught on, after all these centuries? They still believe that ancient deception our ancestors foisted on them. The letter is pronounced "woo," not "vay!" Won't they ever catch on? They continue to be the laughing stock of Europe!"

"And, Wolf…er…Volf…er…Adolph….the voice I heard sounded very Jevish!," Echart proclaimed.

Dietrich continued his report. The voice behind the door went on to say, "And have you heard about that guy named Hitler? He tried to take over the Nazi party by a coup he calls 'The Beer Hall Putsch.' If you ask me, *he's* the putz!"

"Jevish!? Are you trying to tell me that we have been pronouncing "vay" wrong all these generations, and it has been a trick planned by the Jevs!?" Hitler's face reddened, his neck bulged, and he hurled his beer stein across the room, smashing it against the wall.

"This is an unforgiveable insult to all Germans in the vorld....or the world...or, *verdammen*! (damn it!). It's the Jevs. I vill not rest until every Jev across the vorld...I mean world...I mean...."

The Wolf (I mean Volf) went *überschnappen* (fecal-in-the-face ballistic). He tossed Dietrick's coat into his face and demanded he leave at once. As his friend closed the door, he heard behind him, "Get the Jevs....or the Jews...no, the Jevs." How dare they insult the Mother Land! *Deutschland über alles!* (Germany above all!). Get the Jevs!"

Adolph Hitler experienced many insults, verbal attacks, much public humiliation in the years before the birth of the Third Reich. None more devastating, however, than the knowledge those he had fought in Vorld Var Ein had messed with the most treasured asset of any nation: its spoken language. The rest is history.

It is recorded that a handwritten sign was once placed above Hitler's supposed place of death, below the ground, in the Führerbunker (named in honor of his first employer). The sign simply read, *"Putz."* History can now proclaim *"Yiddish über alles!"* (Tough luck, Adolph).

* * * * * * *

"Winnie and Walter"

The following is an anonymous short story, originally published in <u>Everybody's Scrapbook of Curious Facts</u>, edited by Don Lemon, in the late nineteenth century. The story comprises four hundred-seventy nine words all beginning with a W, and using only seventeen hyphenated words.

****

"Warm weather, Walter! Welcome warm weather! We were wishing winter would wane, weren't we?"

"We were well wearied with waiting," whispered Walter wearily. Wan, white, woe-begone was Walter; wayward, willful, worn with weakness, wasted, waxing weaker whenever winter's wild, withering winds were wailing. Wholly without waywardness was Winifred, Walter's wise, womanly watcher, who, with winsome, wooing way, was well-beloved.

"We won't wait, Walter; while weather's warm we'll wander where woodlands wave, won't we?"

Walter's wanton wretchedness wholly waned. "Why, Winnie, we'll walk where we went when we were with Willie; we'll weave wildflower wreaths, watch woodmen working; woodlice, worms wriggling; windmills whirling; watermills wheeling; we will win wild whortleberries, witness wheat winnowed."

Wisbeach woods were wild with wildflowers; warm, westerly winds whispered where willows were waving; wood-pigeons, wrens, woodpeckers were warbling wild woodnotes. Where Wisbeach water-mill's waters, which were wholly waveless, widened, were waterlilies, waxen white. Winifred wove wreaths with woodbine, whitehorn, wallflowers; whilst Walter whittled wooden wedges with willow wands.

Wholly without warning, wild wet winds woke within Wisbeach woods, whistling where Winifred wandered with Walter; weeping willows were wailing weirdly; waging war with wind-tossed waters. Winifred's wary watchfulness waked.

"Walter, we won't wait."

"Which way, Winnie?"

Winifred wavered. "Why, where were we wandering? Wisbeach woods widen whichever way we walk. Where's Wisbeach white wicket, where's Winston's water-mill?"

Wistfully, Walter witnessed Winifred's wonder. "Winnie, Winnie, we were wrong, wholly wrong; wandering within wild ways. Wayfaring weather-beaten waifs, well-nigh worn-out."

Winifred waited where, within wattled woodwork walls, wagons, wheelbarrows, wains were waiting, weighty with withered wood. Walter, warmly wrapped with Winifred's well-worn wadded waterproof, was wailing woefully, wholly wearied. Winnie, who, worn with watching, well-nigh weeping, was wistfully, wakefully waiting Willie's well-known whistle, wholly wished Walter's well-being warranted.

With well-timed wisdom, Walter was wound with wide, worsted wrappers, which wonderfully well withstood winter's withering, whistling winds. Wholly without warm wrappers was Winifred, who, with womanly wisdom, was watching Walter's welfare, warding Walter's weakness.

"When will Willie wend where we wait?" wearily wondered Walter.

"Whist, Walter," whispered Winnie, "who was whooping?"

"Whereabouts?"

Welcome whistling was waking Wisbeach woods when winter's windy warfare waxed weaker.

"Winnie! Walter!"

Winifred's wakefulness was well-grounded. "We're well, Willie; we're where Winston's wagons wait."

Without waiting, Willie was within Winston's woodwork walls.

"Welcome, welcome, Willie." Winnie was weeping with weariness with watching Walter, weak with wayfaring.

"Why Winnie! Wise, watchful, warm-hearted Winnie," Willie whispered wheedlingly. "We won't weep; Walter's well. What were Walter without Winnie?"

Wholly wonderful was Winifred's well-timed womanly wisdom, which well warranted weakly Walter's welfare. Whenever wandering within Wisbeach woods with Winnie, Walter would whisper, "What were Walter without Winnie? Wise, watchful, warm-hearted Winnie!"

NOTES

Unless otherwise noted, all references to words from Old English are taken from the *Oxford English Dictionary, 2ⁿᵈ ed.*, J.A. Simpson and E.S.C. Weiner, editors (New York: Oxford University Press, 1989); and all references to words from Middle English are from *A Concise Dictionary of Middle English*, A.L. Mayhew and Walter William Skeat, (Bibliobazaar, 2006). Bible references are from *New Revised Standard Version* (New York: Division of Christian Education of the National Council of the Churches of Christ in the U.S.A., 1989)

1. Tom McArthur, ed, *Oxford Companion to the English Language*, (New York: Oxford University Press, 1992), 1095.
2. *Merriam-Webster's Collegiate Dictionary; Eleventh Edition* (Springfield, MA: Merriam-Webster, 2003).
3. www.askoxford/asktheexperts/aboutwords.com.
4. See Note #2.
5. Margaret Bryant, *Modern English and Its Heritage*, (New York: McMillan & Co., 1962), 48.
6. Ibid, various chapters.
7. Tom McArthur, 1098.
8. I.J.M.U.T.C.
9. Ibid

10. Bill Bryson, *The Mother Tongue: English and How It Got That Way*, (New York: Wm Morrow & Co., 1990), 84.
11. *Merriam-Webster's*, 266.
12. Tom McArthur, 1095-96.
13. Bill Bryson, 84-85.
14. Tom McArthur, 1099
15. David Sacks, *Language Visible; Unraveling the mystery of the Alphabet from A to Z*, (New York: Broadway Books, 2003), 332.
16. I.J.M.U.T.C
17. Jeremy Marshall and Fred McDonald, eds, *Questions of English*, (New York: Oxford University Press, 1992), 84-85.
18. *Merriam-Webster's*, 35a.
19. www.fonts.com/Templates.
20. www.fonts.com/Templates.
21. David Sacks, 332
22. www.alphabetandletter.com/W
23. Tom McArthur, 1099
24. David Sacks, 334.
25. David Sacks, 332.
26. David Sacks, 331.
27. J.A. Burrow and Thorlac Turville-Petre, *A Book of Middle English, 2nd Edition*, (Cambridge, MA: Blackwell Publishing, 1996), 11.
28. I.J.M.U.T.C.
29. www.en.wikipedia.org/wiki/English_alphabet.
30. *Merriam-Webster's*, 37a
31. www.en.wikipedia.org/wiki/V
32. www.fonts.com/Templates.
33. David Sacks, 335.
34. www.fonts.com/Templates.
35. I.J.M.U.T.C.

36. I.J.M.U.T.C.
37. Ingo R. Titze, *The Human Instrument*, (*Scientific American*, December 2007), as appearing at www.sciam.com/article.
38. www.en.wikipedia.org/Swedish_alphabet.
39. www.en.wikipedia.org/wiki/pronuciationofwww.
40. www.en.wikipedia.org/wiki/linking_and_intrusiveR.
41. "Old English," www.en.wikipedia.org/wiki/English_alphabet.
42. "Letter Frequencies," www.en.wikipedia.org/wiki/English_alphabet.
43. "The National Association of 'W' Lovers Lyrics", www.muppet.wikia.com/wiki/the_national_association_of_W_lovers.
44. c1973 Instructional Children's Music, Inc.; music by Joe Raposo, lyrics by Jerry Juhl.
45. I.J.M.U.T.C.

About the Author

Wallace Whoolery White lives in Delaware, Ohio. He is 5' 8" and weighs a mostly well-proportioned 160 pounds (though one pound in a left haunch is strangely trapezoidal). He wears size 10 shoes, though they are two sizes too big for him. He sports two tattoos, one on his right forearm which reads "Tattoo," the other on the rear of his left shoulder, which says "Shoulder."

He was born in Rowlesburg, W.Va. in 1941, but raised in Marion, Ohio, home of President Warren G. Harding. How that all came about is a bit fuzzy (Harding's election, that is, not White's transfer from W.Va. to Ohio). W. Whoolery has little recollection of the entire year of 1952. To the best of his memory, he was too young to vote for Dwight Eisenhower, so he voted for Adlai Stevenson instead.

He earned a bachelor's degree in English from Miami (OH) University (White, not Harding...*he* attended Iberia College), and a masters in library science at Kent State University. It was there at KSU in the tumultuous '60's that he learned that library work is actually more an art than a science.

Some say White has had a plethora of careers, though they usually mispronounce "plethora." He taught high school English at Marion Harding High School (apparently named for Tonya Harding), followed by three decades in public library administration. Five separate Ohio communities claim him as a one-time member of their library management team, though two of those Ohio cities are lying (Dunquat and Iberia).

Following retirement from public service, he worked as a reporter and copy editor for a couple small town newspapers, and attended seminary. He is a recorded Friends pastor in the Evangelical Friends Church – Eastern Region. W³ finds nothing at all funny about his role as pastor, though he insists God does have a sense of humor. The chief evidence, he suggests, is people who see the image of Mary in a pancake or on a headstone. Absent reliable photos of the mother of Jesus, White believes the imagines usually look more like Betty Davis.

He served 13 years as pastor of Valleyview Evangelical Friends Church in Delaware, OH. Married for 50 years before the passing of his wife in 2013, they were blessed with three children and five grandchildren, all of whom find W³ a bit embarrassing at times.

White sums up his life to this point in this way: "My only regret is that I never learned to yodel."

I.J.M.U.S.T.C. ("I just made up *some* of this crap").

****

wallacewhoolery@columbus.rr.com